KNOW GROWTH

A Guide for Leaders to Identify and Cultivate Students' Spiritual Growth

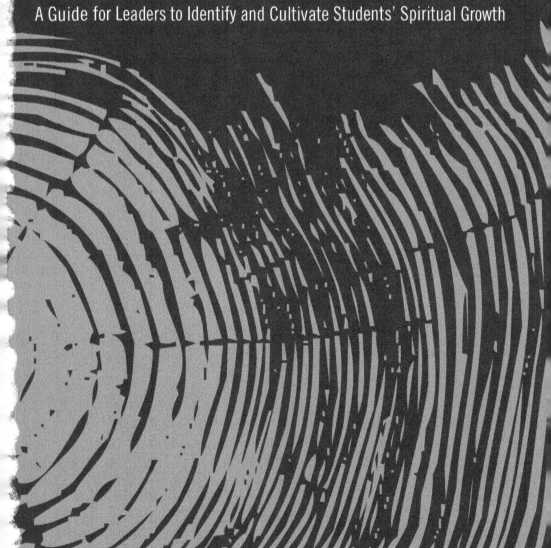

Making Disciples...Developing Leaders

Know Growth: A guide for leaders to identify and cultivate students' spritual growth

Copyright © 2014 by LeaderTreks

ISBN 978-1-939031-118-1

Published by LeaderTreks
25W560 Geneva Road, Suite 30
Carol Stream, IL 60188

www.leadertreks.com
877-502-0699

Table of Contents

Why use Know Growth?...4

How to use this book..5

Student Profile... 5

Growth Plan... 6

Discipleship Map... 8

Student 1...16

Student 2... 26

Student 3... 36

Student 4..46

Student 5... 56

Student 6... 66

Student 7... 76

Student 8... 86

Student 9... 96

Student 10 106

Appendix *(Go Deeper: 8 Discipleship Roots)* 116

KNOW GROWTH

A guide for leaders to identify and cultivate students' spiritual growth.

Why use Know Growth? This book is a tool designed to help you get the most out of relationships with students. So often we think that if we just spend time with a student, we are doing the work of the Lord. Relationship building is important, but it must have a goal. Are you willing to settle for friendship? Or is your goal to lead students into a deeper walk with Jesus? By default students who are rooted disciples of Christ positively influence other students. The goal of this journal is to help you develop strong relationships with students who will make disciples and influence others.

This type of intentional relationship starts with dreaming about the greatest things God will do in your students' lives. Often we in ministry limit God because we forget that he wants to do incredible things through our students. We get caught in the lie that he only wants students not to smoke, drink, or get bad grades. In reality God stands ready to do great things in and through each of his children. This journal will get you thinking about how God is using your students now, and how you can help prepare them for future service. This means helping your students learn to follow him and discover that he has a mission for their lives.

This book is divided into three sections: Student Profile Pages, Discipleship Maps, and Individual Growth Plans.

Who is this for? Are you a small group leader, coach, youth volunteer, or mentor? Are you influencing and investing in students' spiritual growth? Then this book is for you.

When do I use this? This book is best used as a bookend to your time with students—not in a time-consuming, need-to-study kind of way; but in a short-glance-before-meeting-with-a-student way. It will help you focus your time so you'll know where you can whisper support and what challenging questions you can ask. The same is true *after* you spend time with students. Then you can track the growth you see in their lives and pray intentionally for them.

In this book, you'll track students' progression, identifying the fruits of a disciple and discovering challenge areas as well as areas in need of encouragement.

How To Use This Book:
This book comes with space for you to encourage and cultivate 10 students on their discipleship journies. Each student has a *Profile Page*, a *Growth Plan*, and a *Discipleship Map*. As your relationships grow, so do the goals, prayers, and challenges you set for students in the following pages. These pages will morph to accomodate the changes in each student's spiritual journey. And last but not least, mentoring questions, deeper descriptions, and additional Bible passages are included in the back of this book.

STEP 1: STUDENT PROFILE PAGES

The students in whom you are investing are uniquely designed by a *very* creative God, as I'm sure you've figured out. No two are the same, no matter how many stereotypes they fit into. The profile pages are designed to grow in sync with the depth of the relationship you are building with each student. You'll probably fill out the baseline questions about who they are and the activities they are involved in pretty easily. But deeper questions about their families, passions, burdens, and spiritual gifts might take some time to discover. As you think about these things, your ability to pray for, encourage, and walk the road with each student will be enhanced. The trust and intentionality this knowledge brings will give you an opportunity to grow these students into deeply rooted disciples of Christ. So as your relationships grow, keep referring back to each student's profile page and use this knowledge to guide your words, challenges, activities, and prayers on this road.

SAMPLE

Name:

Family life:

Activities:

Passionate about:

Burdened by:

Influenced by:

Testimony:

Spends free time:

STEP 2: GROWTH PLAN

God is working in and through our students. They are in families, on teams, in peer groups, and at schools. God is doing something in their hearts through their circumstances. Unfortunately, God's work often goes unseen or unrecognized. This happens because students get stuck in the minutia of their own lives, and they may not have someone to point it out and whisper in their ear:

"I see God working in you," or "I see God working through you."

The *Growth Plan* page is for you to take note of the things that God is doing. It's divided into different areas of the student's life so you can write down what God is doing *in* and *through* them. As your relationship grows, this page will become more full. If there's an area on this page that you know nothing about, take it as a challenge to get to know your student better. Go to a game or play they are in, ask questions about their family, serve with them at a church event. This will not only help you see more of God's movement in their lives, but it will also help you to challenge them on consistency. One of the biggest struggles for students is being the same person regardless of the place and circumstances. There are many students who know exactly what to say and how to act at church, but they become completely different people at school or work. So get to know your students in a variety of ways and places, and your impact will be much greater.

SAMPLE

	How is God working IN this student?	How is God working THROUGH this student?
Family		
Peers		
Spiritual Gifts & Wiring		
Leadership		

Growth and Goals: *consider these questions for your student*

How can I encourage the work God is doing IN and THROUGH this student?

How can I challenge this student to grow?

What intentional conversation do I need to have with this student?

What short term and long term goals do I have for this student?

What should you do with the info in the *Growth Plan* journal? Well, start by telling the student what you see. In fact, even if you just did that, you would be miles beyond the investment that most people have made in their lives. Students are used to hearing generic encouragement and challenges, but if you were to actually finish the sentences, "I see God working in you in *this* way..." and "I see God working through you in *this* way..." it would be a powerful moment. Luke 10:27 says, "*He answered: "'Love the Lord your God with all your heart and with all your soul and with all your strength and with all your mind* (what's happening *in* you); *and, 'Love your neighbor as yourself'"* (what's happening *through* you). Imagine if someone sat across from you at a coffee shop and answered these questions for your own life. It builds confidence, inspires, and helps students get comfortable in their unique identities and wiring. From there, tell students where you see their growth potential and whisper some challenges in their ear to live out the same love and grace with their little brother as they do their peers. Use this info to set goals for your student and to cast vision for them about how God could be training them for some future kingdom work and where you could see them a year from now. Challenge them to be faithful, courageous, and consistent

As your student grows, this page will morph. New goals will replace challenges that have been achieved. And your prayers will become more specific and intentional.

STEP 3: DISCIPLESHIP MAPS

The reality is heartbreaking. Students once involved in churches and youth groups are walking away from their faith *en masse*. Dozens of books have been written documenting the extensive studies about this phenomenon. Unfortunately, each new statistic reinforces the sad truth. Our students are leaving. Once they hit college, many desert the religion of their youth and uproot their faith. Like seeds planted in rocky soil, they look healthy as they sprout up, but their lifespan is short. They wither away and fall to the wayside because they weren't rooted deep in the soil.

> While no one but the Holy Spirit can transform the heart of a student, we are responsible for reflecting, uncovering, and resembling the truth that saves lives and makes disciples. We offer nudges, whispers, and embraces along the way.

The problem is that we all make assumptions when we disciple students, especially when they have been in the church for a long time, or have grown up in a Christian home. It's easy to assume these students understand the weight of sin (after all, they've memorized the verses) and their need for a Savior. But have we seen repentance or confession as a part of their lives? We may assume they have embraced the gospel, but have we ever seen them stand for their faith, defend it, or explain it beyond a "God loves you" line?

Hopefully the answer is yes, but in many cases that's not true. In discipleship mapping, you'll look at eight core roots of discipleship and identify which roots your students have shown a deep connection with, and on which ones their grip is looser. You won't do this by making sure the topics have been covered in their small group or Sunday School. You'll do this by watching for traces of depth that come out of someone who deeply embraces the truth.

> For example, the natural reaction of someone who deeply understands the truth about God's character is a growing awe and a declining pride. If we see these signs in a student, we can tell which areas of their faith are deeply rooted and which areas need a little more care.

Insight into the depth of a student's faith roots will change the questions you ask them, the truth you speak into their lives, and the challenges you offer them. It can bring a new level of intentionality to your limited time with them and help them become rooted followers of Christ.

**The appendix of this book has additional information, questions to ask, resources to use, and further explanation of each discipleship root.

WARNING: Discipleship mapping is not black and white. Ultimately, only God knows the heart of a student, only he can measure faith. This tool is designed to give you clues and signifiers that allow you to dive intentionally into a student's life; to ask questions that lead to growth and to offer road signs that help guide students toward Christ. In the same way that church participation in small groups can be a sign of church health, it is not a measurement of faith. Only God holds that measuring stick. Discipleship mapping simply looks for signs and clues that give us a direction to take our students.

SAMPLE DISCIPLESHIP MAP

1. Check the boxes of words or phrases in both columns that represent or describe your student. If you are unsure or don't know this student in a particular area, then feel free to leave the box empty.
2. When you are finished, look at which of the eight areas (Rescue, Identity, and so on) show a lot of depth—many items checked on the left side and few on the right. Consider how you can encourage or support this student in those areas (an encouragement note, text, or even pointing them to an opportunity where they could continue to grow deeper).
3. Next, decipher which of the eight areas is a struggle for your student, where the warning signs are greatly mounted against the traces of depth. Consider how you might challenge and come alongside your student. A great place to start is with prayer (check out the prayer page for each student) and by adding step-by-step goals or challenges to the appropriate Growth Plan.

Go Deeper in two ways!
1. In the appendix of this book (page 116) you'll find suggestions on how to help students grow in each of these eight areas, as well as extra definitions, key Scriptures, and intentional questions.

2. *I Am A Disciple:* Consider purchasing this book for your student to spend **40 days of practical daily devotionals and experiences** to learn about and grow as a disciple. This journal will cover many of the "marks" of a disciple, go deeply into the eight core roots, and include mentor pages for you to use as you walk alongside your student's discipleship journey.

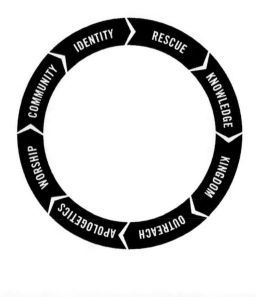

RESCUE: Students who are deeply rooted in their story of being rescued by Christ (salvation and redemption) often show these traces of depth. Students who might not completely grasp this part of discipleship show these warning signs. Check the boxes of words or phrases in both columns that reflect your student's lifestyle.

*For a more complete definition of "Rescue," Scripture verses, as well as some questions to guide a student in their discipleship journey related to this area (and all eight discipleship areas), check out the appendix on page 116.

TRACES OF DEPTH	WARNING SIGNS
❏ passion for evangelism	❏ works-based faith
❏ thankfulness	❏ tries to earn God's love
❏ sacrifices for God and/or others	❏ points fingers
❏ uncompromising	❏ holds onto guilt and shame
❏ lifestyle consistency (same person in all places and circumstances)	❏ holds grudges
❏ confession/repentance is a part of their life	❏ keeps score
❏ offers forgiveness	❏ makes excuses
❏ shows grace to others and self	❏ acts entitled
❏ a realized need for a Savior	❏ blames others often
❏ understands consequences of sin	❏ takes God's grace for granted

KNOWLEDGE: Students who are deeply rooted in the truth about who God is and their pursuit of knowing him often show these traces of depth. Students who might hold a false sense of God, or haven't pursued knowing God may display these warning signs. (Go deeper on page 118.)

TRACES OF DEPTH	WARNING SIGNS
❏ a growing awe	❏ growing pride
❏ healthy fear of God	❏ acknowledges more than one God
❏ value for God's Word	❏ hides from God
❏ knows the God of the Bible	❏ foolishness
❏ humility/self-awareness	❏ lacks value for God's word
❏ growing love/desire to know him	❏ apathy
❏ worshipful lifestyle	❏ seeks beyond God
❏ God is a part of decisions	❏ anger at God
❏ relationship with God exists beyond the church walls	❏ expects God to have no involvement
❏ reflects wisdom	❏ makes him/herself God of their life

IDENTITY:
Students who are deeply rooted in their identity as God's children often show some of these traces of depth. Students who struggle to know or live out this identity may display some of these warning signs. (Go deeper on page 120.)

TRACES OF DEPTH	WARNING SIGNS
❏ confidence and self-awareness	❏ puts others down
❏ using spiritual gifts and wiring/personality for the kingdom	❏ identity or worth is determined by environment (performance, teams, groups, problems, etc.)
❏ consistent lifestyle (same person in all circumstances)	❏ trying to be someone they aren't
❏ comfortable in their own skin	❏ fear or insecurity
❏ affirming of others	❏ self-deprecating
❏ likes who they are	❏ consumed with outer appearance
❏ embraces growth	❏ depression/anxiety
❏ accepts criticism	❏ works to feed ego or people pleaser
❏ honest	❏ social media identity doesn't match reality
❏ accepts and seeks help	❏ me against the world mentality

KINGDOM:
Students who are deeply rooted in their understanding of God's kingdom and who are living from a kingdom perspective often show some of these traces of depth. Students who struggle to embrace this perspective and are wrestling with a worldly or cultural perspective may display some of these warning signs.
(Go deeper on page 122.)

TRACES OF DEPTH	WARNING SIGNS
❏ inspired to serve	❏ driven by materialism
❏ embracing the last and least	❏ rarely steps outside of comfort zone
❏ pushes their comfort zone	❏ one-upmanship
❏ willing to sacrifice	❏ selfish
❏ appreciation for current circumstances	❏ lives in the moment
❏ welcoming and inclusive of others	❏ sees themselves as king of their life
❏ selfless	❏ reckless living
❏ has a long-term perspective	❏ rarely sees ways to serve others
❏ knows the King	❏ has many "idols" before God
❏ regularly gives without payment (time, money, attention, resources, respect)	❏ easily overwhelmed by short-term obstacles

OUTREACH: Students who are deeply rooted in their desire and ability to reach the lost show some of these traces of depth. Students who struggle to reach out to the lost may display some of these warning signs. (Go deeper on page 124.)

TRACES OF DEPTH	WARNING SIGNS
❑ inspired to serve ❑ seeks out the lost ❑ willing to share their faith story ❑ burden for the lost ❑ uses current situations as outreach (where and who they already are) ❑ gives sacrificially (time, money, gifts, etc.) ❑ deep value for others (beyond friends) ❑ courageously shares God's truth ❑ has positive influence on the lost ❑ desire for justice in the world	❑ selfish ❑ uses people ❑ does things that devalue people ❑ afraid to talk about spiritual things ❑ patronizing/mocking ❑ makes excuses for not reaching out ❑ fear of judgment ❑ unsure of spiritual truth ❑ apathetic ❑ easily influenced by the lost

WORSHIP: Students who are deeply rooted in a lifestyle of worship show some of these traces of depth. Students who struggle to worship or show adoration may display some of these warning signs. (Go deeper on page 126.)

TRACES OF DEPTH	WARNING SIGNS
❑ faith is part of their whole life ❑ drawn to worship ❑ gives freely/initiates giving ❑ obedience to God ❑ prayer is a staple and spontaneous ❑ comfortable praying in groups/out loud ❑ thankfulness ❑ desire to imitate Christ/God ❑ worships regardless of circumstance ❑ joyful	❑ many idols (things they value higher than God) ❑ showy worship ❑ takes things for granted ❑ many spiritual highs and lows ❑ feeling-based faith/worship ❑ overly critical of worship styles ❑ shallow prayer life ❑ only worships by singing ❑ worship is compartmentalized to church ❑ sacrifices begrudgingly

APOLOGETICS: Students who are deeply rooted in the truths that sustain their faith show some of these traces of depth. Students who struggle to know and own the truth of their faith may show some of these warning signs. (Go deeper on page 128.)

TRACES OF DEPTH	WARNING SIGNS
❏ balances knowing God and knowing about God ❏ able to communicate faith story ❏ has spiritual mentors ❏ honest (especially about doubt or unknowns) ❏ humble ❏ willingness to learn/teachable ❏ has a recognizable faith ❏ lovingly holds that Christ is the only way ❏ speaks truth in love ❏ high value for the Bible	❏ combative/argumentative ❏ unteachable ❏ believes all opinions on God are true ❏ thinks they have it all figured out ❏ is okay with many higher powers as true ❏ disregards the Bible ❏ derailed by doubt ❏ cannot articulate their faith ❏ beliefs are easily swayed ❏ lacks spiritual mentoring

COMMUNITY: Students who are deeply rooted in their connection with the community of Christ show some of these traces of depth. Students who struggle to be a part of Christian community may display some of these warning signs. (Go deeper on page 130.)

TRACES OF DEPTH	WARNING SIGNS
❏ has many kinds of relationships (mentor, accountability, mentee, outreach) ❏ peacemaker ❏ encourager ❏ submits to spiritual authority ❏ inclusive/welcoming ❏ promotes unity in the church/youth group ❏ understands their role to minister to the world ❏ authentic living—represents the church in or outside of the building ❏ knows/uses spiritual gifts ❏ serving in the church	❏ isolation ❏ holding grudges ❏ avoiding ❏ gossip ❏ divisive ❏ exclusive ❏ inconsistent lifestyle/attitude and actions ❏ constant critic ❏ parasitic ❏ expecting church to serve them

PRAYER:

After you spend time in any of these three areas (Student Profile, Discipleship Map, or Vision Plan), use the prayer pages to guide your prayers for this student and your relationship. Also, use these pages to keep a record of the prayers God has answered. The intentionality and power of this discipleship relationship will increase when you make prayer a regular part of it.

ANSWERS TO PRAYER:

Student Name

[   ]

So then, just as you received Christ Jesus
as Lord, **continue to live your lives in him**,
ROOTED AND BUILT UP IN HIM, strengthened in
the faith as you were taught, and overflowing
with thankfulness. **Colossians 2:6–7**

Student Profile

Name:

Family life:

Activities:

Passionate about:

Burdened by:

Influenced by:

Testimony:

Spends free time:

Growth Plan

	PERSONAL GROWTH: How is God working **IN** this student?	MINISTRY GROWTH: How is God working **THROUGH** this student?
Family		
Peers		
Spiritual Gifts & Wiring		
Leadership		

Growth Plan

GROWTH AND GOALS: consider these questions for your student

How can I encourage the work God is doing IN and THROUGH this student?

How can I challenge this student to grow?

What intentional conversation do I need to have with this student?

What short term and long term goals do I have for this student?

DISCIPLESHIP MAP

1. Check the boxes of words or phrases in both columns that represent or describe your student. If you are unsure or don't know this student in a particular area, then feel free to leave the box empty.
2. When you are finished, look at which of the eight areas (Rescue, Identity, and so on) show a lot of depth—many items checked on the left side and few on the right. Consider how you can encourage or support this student in those areas (an encouragement note, text, or even pointing them to an opportunity where they could continue to grow deeper).
3. Next, decipher which of the eight areas is a struggle for your student, where the warning signs are greatly mounted against the traces of depth. Consider how you might challenge and come alongside your student. A great place to start is with prayer (check out the prayer page for each student) and by adding step-by-step goals or challenges to the Growth Plan (page 18).

RESCUE: Students who are deeply rooted in their story of being rescued by Christ (salvation and redemption) often show these traces of depth. Students who might not completely grasp this part of discipleship show these warning signs. Check the boxes of words or phrases in both columns that reflect your student's lifestyle.

*For a more complete definition of "Rescue," Scripture verses, as well as some questions to guide a student in their discipleship journey related to this area (and all eight discipleship areas), check out the appendix on page 116.

TRACES OF DEPTH	WARNING SIGNS
❏ passion for evangelism	❏ works-based faith
❏ thankfulness	❏ tries to earn God's love
❏ sacrifices for God and/or others	❏ points fingers
❏ uncompromising	❏ holds onto guilt and shame
❏ lifestyle consistency (same person in all places and circumstances)	❏ holds grudges
	❏ keeps score
❏ confession/repentance is a part of their life	❏ makes excuses
❏ offers forgiveness	❏ acts entitled
❏ shows grace to others and self	❏ blames others often
❏ a realized need for a Savior	❏ takes God's grace for granted
❏ understands consequences of sin	

KNOWLEDGE: Students who are deeply rooted in the truth about who God is and their pursuit of knowing him often show these traces of depth. Students who might hold a false sense of God, or haven't pursued knowing God may display these warning signs. (Go deeper on page 118.)

TRACES OF DEPTH	WARNING SIGNS
❏ a growing awe	❏ growing pride
❏ healthy fear of God	❏ acknowledges more than one God
❏ value for God's Word	
❏ knows the God of the Bible	❏ hides from God
❏ humility/self-awareness	❏ foolishness
❏ growing love/desire to know him	❏ lacks value for God's word
❏ worshipful lifestyle	❏ apathy
❏ God is a part of decisions	❏ seeks beyond God
❏ relationship with God exists beyond the church walls	❏ anger at God
❏ reflects wisdom	❏ expects God to have no involvement
	❏ makes him/herself God of their life

21

IDENTITY: Students who are deeply rooted in their identity as God's children often show some of these traces of depth. Students who struggle to know or live out this identity may display some of these warning signs. (Go deeper on page 120.)

TRACES OF DEPTH	WARNING SIGNS
❏ confidence and self-awareness ❏ using spiritual gifts and wiring/personality for the kingdom ❏ consistent lifestyle (same person in all circumstances) ❏ comfortable in their own skin ❏ affirming of others ❏ likes who they are ❏ embraces growth ❏ accepts criticism ❏ honest ❏ accepts and seeks help	❏ puts others down ❏ identity or worth is determined by environment (performance, teams, groups, problems, etc.) ❏ trying to be someone they aren't ❏ fear or insecurity ❏ self-deprecating ❏ consumed with outer appearance ❏ depression/anxiety ❏ works to feed ego or people pleaser ❏ social media identity doesn't match reality ❏ me against the world mentality

KINGDOM: Students who are deeply rooted in their understanding of God's kingdom and who are living from a kingdom perspective often show some of these traces of depth. Students who struggle to embrace this perspective and are wrestling with a worldly or cultural perspective may display some of these warning signs.
(Go deeper on page 122.)

TRACES OF DEPTH	WARNING SIGNS
❏ inspired to serve ❏ embracing the last and least ❏ pushes their comfort zone ❏ willing to sacrifice ❏ appreciation for current circumstances ❏ welcoming and inclusive of others ❏ selfless ❏ has a long-term perspective ❏ knows the King ❏ regularly gives without payment (time, money, attention, resources, respect)	❏ driven by materialism ❏ rarely steps outside of comfort zone ❏ one-upmanship ❏ selfish ❏ lives in the moment ❏ sees themselves as king of their life ❏ reckless living ❏ rarely sees ways to serve others ❏ has many "idols" before God ❏ easily overwhelmed by short-term obstacles

OUTREACH: Students who are deeply rooted in their desire and ability to reach the lost show some of these traces of depth. Students who struggle to reach out to the lost may display some of these warning signs. (Go deeper on page 124.)

TRACES OF DEPTH	WARNING SIGNS
❏ inspired to serve ❏ seeks out the lost ❏ willing to share their faith story ❏ burden for the lost ❏ uses current situations as outreach (where and who they already are) ❏ gives sacrificially (time, money, gifts, etc.) ❏ deep value for others (beyond friends) ❏ courageously shares God's truth ❏ has positive influence on the lost ❏ desire for justice in the world	❏ selfish ❏ uses people ❏ does things that devalue people ❏ afraid to talk about spiritual things ❏ patronizing/mocking ❏ makes excuses for not reaching out ❏ fear of judgment ❏ unsure of spiritual truth ❏ apathetic ❏ easily influenced by the lost

WORSHIP: Students who are deeply rooted in a lifestyle of worship show some of these traces of depth. Students who struggle to worship or show adoration may display some of these warning signs. (Go deeper on page 126.)

TRACES OF DEPTH	WARNING SIGNS
❏ faith is part of their whole life ❏ drawn to worship ❏ gives freely/initiates giving ❏ obedience to God ❏ prayer is a staple and spontaneous ❏ comfortable praying in groups/out loud ❏ thankfulness ❏ desire to imitate Christ/God ❏ worships regardless of circumstance ❏ joyful	❏ many idols (things they value higher than God) ❏ showy worship ❏ takes things for granted ❏ many spiritual highs and lows ❏ feeling-based faith/worship ❏ overly critical of worship styles ❏ shallow prayer life ❏ only worships by singing ❏ worship is compartmentalized to church ❏ sacrifices begrudgingly

APOLOGETICS: Students who are deeply rooted in the truths that sustain their faith show some of these traces of depth. Students who struggle to know and own the truth of their faith may show some of these warning signs. (Go deeper on page 128.)

TRACES OF DEPTH	WARNING SIGNS
❏ balances knowing God and knowing about God	❏ combative/argumentative
❏ able to communicate faith story	❏ unteachable
❏ has spiritual mentors	❏ believes all opinions on God are true
❏ honest (especially about doubt or unknowns)	❏ thinks they have it all figured out
❏ humble	❏ is okay with many higher powers as true
❏ willingness to learn/teachable	❏ disregards the Bible
❏ has a recognizable faith	❏ derailed by doubt
❏ lovingly holds that Christ is the only way	❏ cannot articulate their faith
❏ speaks truth in love	❏ beliefs are easily swayed
❏ high value for the Bible	❏ lacks spiritual mentoring

COMMUNITY: Students who are deeply rooted in their connection with the community of Christ show some of these traces of depth. Students who struggle to be a part of Christian community may display some of these warning signs. (Go deeper on page 130.)

TRACES OF DEPTH	WARNING SIGNS
❏ has many kinds of relationships (mentor, accountability, mentee, outreach)	❏ isolation
❏ peacemaker	❏ holding grudges
❏ encourager	❏ avoiding
❏ submits to spiritual authority	❏ gossip
❏ inclusive/welcoming	❏ divisive
❏ promotes unity in the church/youth group	❏ exclusive
❏ understands their role to minister to the world	❏ inconsistent lifestyle/attitude and actions
❏ authentic living—represents the church in or outside of the building	❏ constant critic
❏ knows/uses spiritual gifts	❏ parasitic
❏ serving in the church	❏ expecting church to serve them

Prayer:

Answers to prayer:

2

[ ]

Until you have **given up your self to Him** you will not have a real self.
–C.S. Lewis *(Mere Christianity)*

Student Profile

Name: _____

Family life:

_____

Activities:

_____

Passionate about:

_____

Burdened by:

_____

Influenced by:

_____

Testimony:

_____

Spends free time:

Growth Plan

	PERSONAL GROWTH: How is God working **IN** this student?	MINISTRY GROWTH: How is God working **THROUGH** this student?
Family		
Peers		
Spiritual Gifts & Wiring		
Leadership		

Growth Plan

GROWTH AND GOALS: consider these questions for your student

How can I encourage the work God is doing IN and
THROUGH this student?

How can I challenge this student to grow?

What intentional conversation do I need to have
with this student?

What short term and long term goals do I have for
this student?

DISCIPLESHIP MAP

1. Check the boxes of words or phrases in both columns that represent or describe your student. If you are unsure or don't know this student in a particular area, then feel free to leave the box empty.
2. When you are finished, look at which of the eight areas (Rescue, Identity, and so on) show a lot of depth—many items checked on the left side and few on the right. Consider how you can encourage or support this student in those areas (an encouragement note, text, or even pointing them to an opportunity where they could continue to grow deeper).
3. Next, decipher which of the eight areas is a struggle for your student, where the warning signs are greatly mounted against the traces of depth. Consider how you might challenge and come alongside your student. A great place to start is with prayer (check out the prayer page for each student) and by adding step-by-step goals or challenges to the Growth Plan (page 28).

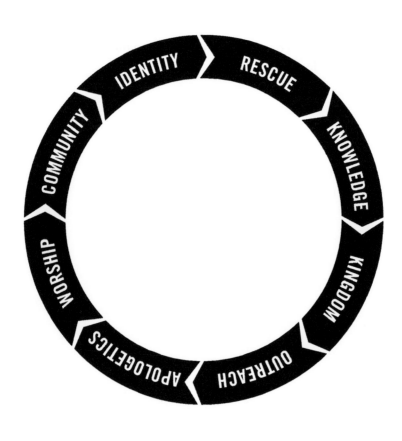

RESCUE: Students who are deeply rooted in their story of being rescued by Christ (salvation and redemption) often show these traces of depth. Students who might not completely grasp this part of discipleship show these warning signs. Check the boxes of words or phrases in both columns that reflect your student's lifestyle.

*For a more complete definition of "Rescue," Scripture verses, as well as some questions to guide a student in their discipleship journey related to this area (and all eight discipleship areas), check out the appendix on page 116.

TRACES OF DEPTH	WARNING SIGNS
❏ passion for evangelism	❏ works-based faith
❏ thankfulness	❏ tries to earn God's love
❏ sacrifices for God and/or others	❏ points fingers
❏ uncompromising	❏ holds onto guilt and shame
❏ lifestyle consistency (same person in all places and circumstances)	❏ holds grudges
	❏ keeps score
❏ confession/repentance is a part of their life	❏ makes excuses
❏ offers forgiveness	❏ acts entitled
❏ shows grace to others and self	❏ blames others often
❏ a realized need for a Savior	❏ takes God's grace for granted
❏ understands consequences of sin	

KNOWLEDGE: Students who are deeply rooted in the truth about who God is and their pursuit of knowing him often show these traces of depth. Students who might hold a false sense of God, or haven't pursued knowing God may display these warning signs. (Go deeper on page 118.)

TRACES OF DEPTH	WARNING SIGNS
❏ a growing awe	❏ growing pride
❏ healthy fear of God	❏ acknowledges more than one God
❏ value for God's Word	
❏ knows the God of the Bible	❏ hides from God
❏ humility/self-awareness	❏ foolishness
❏ growing love/desire to know him	❏ lacks value for God's word
❏ worshipful lifestyle	❏ apathy
❏ God is a part of decisions	❏ seeks beyond God
❏ relationship with God exists beyond the church walls	❏ anger at God
❏ reflects wisdom	❏ expects God to have no involvement
	❏ makes him/herself God of their life

IDENTITY: Students who are deeply rooted in their identity as God's children often show some of these traces of depth. Students who struggle to know or live out this identity may display some of these warning signs. (Go deeper on page 120.)

TRACES OF DEPTH	WARNING SIGNS
❏ confidence and self-awareness ❏ using spiritual gifts and wiring/personality for the kingdom ❏ consistent lifestyle (same person in all circumstances) ❏ comfortable in their own skin ❏ affirming of others ❏ likes who they are ❏ embraces growth ❏ accepts criticism ❏ honest ❏ accepts and seeks help	❏ puts others down ❏ identity or worth is determined by environment (performance, teams, groups, problems, etc.) ❏ trying to be someone they aren't ❏ fear or insecurity ❏ self-deprecating ❏ consumed with outer appearance ❏ depression/anxiety ❏ works to feed ego or people pleaser ❏ social media identity doesn't match reality ❏ me against the world mentality

KINGDOM: Students who are deeply rooted in their understanding of God's kingdom and who are living from a kingdom perspective often show some of these traces of depth. Students who struggle to embrace this perspective and are wrestling with a worldly or cultural perspective may display some of these warning signs.
(Go deeper on page 122.)

TRACES OF DEPTH	WARNING SIGNS
❏ inspired to serve ❏ embracing the last and least ❏ pushes their comfort zone ❏ willing to sacrifice ❏ appreciation for current circumstances ❏ welcoming and inclusive of others ❏ selfless ❏ has a long-term perspective ❏ knows the King ❏ regularly gives without payment (time, money, attention, resources, respect)	❏ driven by materialism ❏ rarely steps outside of comfort zone ❏ one-upmanship ❏ selfish ❏ lives in the moment ❏ sees themselves as king of their life ❏ reckless living ❏ rarely sees ways to serve others ❏ has many "idols" before God ❏ easily overwhelmed by short-term obstacles

OUTREACH: Students who are deeply rooted in their desire and ability to reach the lost show some of these traces of depth. Students who struggle to reach out to the lost may display some of these warning signs. (Go deeper on page 124.)

TRACES OF DEPTH	WARNING SIGNS
❏ inspired to serve ❏ seeks out the lost ❏ willing to share their faith story ❏ burden for the lost ❏ uses current situations as outreach (where and who they already are) ❏ gives sacrificially (time, money, gifts, etc.) ❏ deep value for others (beyond friends) ❏ courageously shares God's truth ❏ has positive influence on the lost ❏ desire for justice in the world	❏ selfish ❏ uses people ❏ does things that devalue people ❏ afraid to talk about spiritual things ❏ patronizing/mocking ❏ makes excuses for not reaching out ❏ fear of judgment ❏ unsure of spiritual truth ❏ apathetic ❏ easily influenced by the lost

WORSHIP: Students who are deeply rooted in a lifestyle of worship show some of these traces of depth. Students who struggle to worship or show adoration may display some of these warning signs. (Go deeper on page 126.)

TRACES OF DEPTH	WARNING SIGNS
❏ faith is part of their whole life ❏ drawn to worship ❏ gives freely/initiates giving ❏ obedience to God ❏ prayer is a staple and spontaneous ❏ comfortable praying in groups/out loud ❏ thankfulness ❏ desire to imitate Christ/God ❏ worships regardless of circumstance ❏ joyful	❏ many idols (things they value higher than God) ❏ showy worship ❏ takes things for granted ❏ many spiritual highs and lows ❏ feeling-based faith/worship ❏ overly critical of worship styles ❏ shallow prayer life ❏ only worships by singing ❏ worship is compartmentalized to church ❏ sacrifices begrudgingly

APOLOGETICS: Students who are deeply rooted in the truths that sustain their faith show some of these traces of depth. Students who struggle to know and own the truth of their faith may show some of these warning signs. (Go deeper on page 128.)

TRACES OF DEPTH	WARNING SIGNS
❏ balances knowing God and knowing about God ❏ able to communicate faith story ❏ has spiritual mentors ❏ honest (especially about doubt or unknowns) ❏ humble ❏ willingness to learn/teachable ❏ has a recognizable faith ❏ lovingly holds that Christ is the only way ❏ speaks truth in love ❏ high value for the Bible	❏ combative/argumentative ❏ unteachable ❏ believes all opinions on God are true ❏ thinks they have it all figured out ❏ is okay with many higher powers as true ❏ disregards the Bible ❏ derailed by doubt ❏ cannot articulate their faith ❏ beliefs are easily swayed ❏ lacks spiritual mentoring

COMMUNITY: Students who are deeply rooted in their connection with the community of Christ show some of these traces of depth. Students who struggle to be a part of Christian community may display some of these warning signs. (Go deeper on page 130.)

TRACES OF DEPTH	WARNING SIGNS
❏ has many kinds of relationships (mentor, accountability, mentee, outreach) ❏ peacemaker ❏ encourager ❏ submits to spiritual authority ❏ inclusive/welcoming ❏ promotes unity in the church/youth group ❏ understands their role to minister to the world ❏ authentic living—represents the church in or outside of the building ❏ knows/uses spiritual gifts ❏ serving in the church	❏ isolation ❏ holding grudges ❏ avoiding ❏ gossip ❏ divisive ❏ exclusive ❏ inconsistent lifestyle/attitude and actions ❏ constant critic ❏ parasitic ❏ expecting church to serve them

Prayer:

Answers to prayer:

Student Name

3

[   ]

If you REMAIN IN ME and my words remain
in you, **ask whatever you wish**, and it will
be given you. THIS IS TO MY FATHER'S GLORY,
that you bear much fruit, showing yourselves
TO BE MY DISCIPLES. **John 15:8**

Student Profile

Name: _____

Family life:

_____

Activities:

_____

Passionate about:

_____

Burdened by:

_____

Influenced by:

_____

Testimony:

_____

Spends free time:

Growth Plan

	PERSONAL GROWTH: How is God working **IN** this student?	MINISTRY GROWTH: How is God working **THROUGH** this student?
Family		
Peers		
Spiritual Gifts & Wiring		
Leadership		

Growth Plan

GROWTH AND GOALS: consider these questions for your student

How can I encourage the work God is doing IN and THROUGH this student?

3

How can I challenge this student to grow?

What intentional conversation do I need to have with this student?

What short term and long term goals do I have for this student?

DISCIPLESHIP MAP

1. Check the boxes of words or phrases in both columns that represent or describe your student. If you are unsure or don't know this student in a particular area, then feel free to leave the box empty.
2. When you are finished, look at which of the eight areas (Rescue, Identity, and so on) show a lot of depth—many items checked on the left side and few on the right. Consider how you can encourage or support this student in those areas (an encouragement note, text, or even pointing them to an opportunity where they could continue to grow deeper).
3. Next, decipher which of the eight areas is a struggle for your student, where the warning signs are greatly mounted against the traces of depth. Consider how you might challenge and come alongside your student. A great place to start is with prayer (check out the prayer page for each student) and by adding step-by-step goals or challenges to the Growth Plan (page 38).

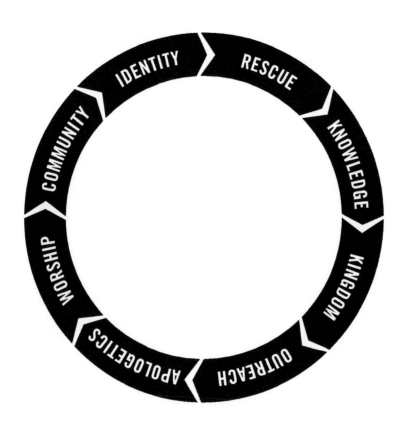

RESCUE: Students who are deeply rooted in their story of being rescued by Christ (salvation and redemption) often show these traces of depth. Students who might not completely grasp this part of discipleship show these warning signs. Check the boxes of words or phrases in both columns that reflect your student's lifestyle.

*For a more complete definition of "Rescue," Scripture verses, as well as some questions to guide a student in their discipleship journey related to this area (and all eight discipleship areas), check out the appendix on page 116.

TRACES OF DEPTH	WARNING SIGNS
❏ passion for evangelism	❏ works-based faith
❏ thankfulness	❏ tries to earn God's love
❏ sacrifices for God and/or others	❏ points fingers
❏ uncompromising	❏ holds onto guilt and shame
❏ lifestyle consistency (same person in all places and circumstances)	❏ holds grudges
	❏ keeps score
❏ confession/repentance is a part of their life	❏ makes excuses
❏ offers forgiveness	❏ acts entitled
❏ shows grace to others and self	❏ blames others often
❏ a realized need for a Savior	❏ takes God's grace for granted
❏ understands consequences of sin	

KNOWLEDGE: Students who are deeply rooted in the truth about who God is and their pursuit of knowing him often show these traces of depth. Students who might hold a false sense of God, or haven't pursued knowing God may display these warning signs. (Go deeper on page 118.)

TRACES OF DEPTH	WARNING SIGNS
❏ a growing awe	❏ growing pride
❏ healthy fear of God	❏ acknowledges more than one God
❏ value for God's Word	
❏ knows the God of the Bible	❏ hides from God
❏ humility/self-awareness	❏ foolishness
❏ growing love/desire to know him	❏ lacks value for God's word
❏ worshipful lifestyle	❏ apathy
❏ God is a part of decisions	❏ seeks beyond God
❏ relationship with God exists beyond the church walls	❏ anger at God
❏ reflects wisdom	❏ expects God to have no involvement
	❏ makes him/herself God of their life

3

IDENTITY: Students who are deeply rooted in their identity as God's children often show some of these traces of depth. Students who struggle to know or live out this identity may display some of these warning signs. (Go deeper on page 120.)

(Go deeper on page 120.)

TRACES OF DEPTH	WARNING SIGNS
❏ confidence and self-awareness	❏ puts others down
❏ using spiritual gifts and wiring/personality for the kingdom	❏ identity or worth is determined by environment (performance, teams, groups, problems, etc.)
❏ consistent lifestyle (same person in all circumstances)	❏ trying to be someone they aren't
❏ comfortable in their own skin	❏ fear or insecurity
❏ affirming of others	❏ self-deprecating
❏ likes who they are	❏ consumed with outer appearance
❏ embraces growth	❏ depression/anxiety
❏ accepts criticism	❏ works to feed ego or people pleaser
❏ honest	❏ social media identity doesn't match reality
❏ accepts and seeks help	❏ me against the world mentality

KINGDOM: Students who are deeply rooted in their understanding of God's kingdom and who are living from a kingdom perspective often show some of these traces of depth. Students who struggle to embrace this perspective and are wrestling with a worldly or cultural perspective may display some of these warning signs.
(Go deeper on page 122.)

(Go deeper on page 122.)

TRACES OF DEPTH	WARNING SIGNS
❏ inspired to serve	❏ driven by materialism
❏ embracing the last and least	❏ rarely steps outside of comfort zone
❏ pushes their comfort zone	❏ one-upmanship
❏ willing to sacrifice	❏ selfish
❏ appreciation for current circumstances	❏ lives in the moment
❏ welcoming and inclusive of others	❏ sees themselves as king of their life
❏ selfless	❏ reckless living
❏ has a long-term perspective	❏ rarely sees ways to serve others
❏ knows the King	❏ has many "idols" before God
❏ regularly gives without payment (time, money, attention, resources, respect)	❏ easily overwhelmed by short-term obstacles

3

OUTREACH: Students who are deeply rooted in their desire and ability to reach the lost show some of these traces of depth. Students who struggle to reach out to the lost may display some of these warning signs. (Go deeper on page 124.)

TRACES OF DEPTH	WARNING SIGNS
❏ inspired to serve ❏ seeks out the lost ❏ willing to share their faith story ❏ burden for the lost ❏ uses current situations as outreach (where and who they already are) ❏ gives sacrificially (time, money, gifts, etc.) ❏ deep value for others (beyond friends) ❏ courageously shares God's truth ❏ has positive influence on the lost ❏ desire for justice in the world	❏ selfish ❏ uses people ❏ does things that devalue people ❏ afraid to talk about spiritual things ❏ patronizing/mocking ❏ makes excuses for not reaching out ❏ fear of judgment ❏ unsure of spiritual truth ❏ apathetic ❏ easily influenced by the lost

3

WORSHIP: Students who are deeply rooted in a lifestyle of worship show some of these traces of depth. Students who struggle to worship or show adoration may display some of these warning signs. (Go deeper on page 126.)

TRACES OF DEPTH	WARNING SIGNS
❏ faith is part of their whole life ❏ drawn to worship ❏ gives freely/initiates giving ❏ obedience to God ❏ prayer is a staple and spontaneous ❏ comfortable praying in groups/out loud ❏ thankfulness ❏ desire to imitate Christ/God ❏ worships regardless of circumstance ❏ joyful	❏ many idols (things they value higher than God) ❏ showy worship ❏ takes things for granted ❏ many spiritual highs and lows ❏ feeling-based faith/worship ❏ overly critical of worship styles ❏ shallow prayer life ❏ only worships by singing ❏ worship is compartmentalized to church ❏ sacrifices begrudgingly

APOLOGETICS: Students who are deeply rooted in the truths that sustain their faith show some of these traces of depth. Students who struggle to know and own the truth of their faith may show some of these warning signs. (Go deeper on page 128.)

TRACES OF DEPTH	WARNING SIGNS
❏ balances knowing God and knowing about God ❏ able to communicate faith story ❏ has spiritual mentors ❏ honest (especially about doubt or unknowns) ❏ humble ❏ willingness to learn/teachable ❏ has a recognizable faith ❏ lovingly holds that Christ is the only way ❏ speaks truth in love ❏ high value for the Bible	❏ combative/argumentative ❏ unteachable ❏ believes all opinions on God are true ❏ thinks they have it all figured out ❏ is okay with many higher powers as true ❏ disregards the Bible ❏ derailed by doubt ❏ cannot articulate their faith ❏ beliefs are easily swayed ❏ lacks spiritual mentoring

COMMUNITY: Students who are deeply rooted in their connection with the community of Christ show some of these traces of depth. Students who struggle to be a part of Christian community may display some of these warning signs. (Go deeper on page 130.)

TRACES OF DEPTH	WARNING SIGNS
❏ has many kinds of relationships (mentor, accountability, mentee, outreach) ❏ peacemaker ❏ encourager ❏ submits to spiritual authority ❏ inclusive/welcoming ❏ promotes unity in the church/youth group ❏ understands their role to minister to the world ❏ authentic living—represents the church in or outside of the building ❏ knows/uses spiritual gifts ❏ serving in the church	❏ isolation ❏ holding grudges ❏ avoiding ❏ gossip ❏ divisive ❏ exclusive ❏ inconsistent lifestyle/attitude and actions ❏ constant critic ❏ parasitic ❏ expecting church to serve them

Prayer:

Answers to prayer:

Student Name

[   ]

When we are CALLED TO FOLLOW CHRIST,
we are summoned to an **exclusive attachment**
to his person. —Dietrich Bonhoeffer

(The Cost of Discipleship)

Student Profile

Name: _____

Family life: _____

_____

Activities: _____

_____

Passionate about: _____

_____

Burdened by: _____

_____

Influenced by: _____

_____

Testimony: _____

_____

Spends free time:

Growth Plan

	PERSONAL GROWTH: How is God working **IN** this student?	MINISTRY GROWTH: How is God working **THROUGH** this student?
Family		
Peers		
Spiritual Gifts & Wiring		
Leadership		

Growth Plan

GROWTH AND GOALS: consider these questions for your student

How can I encourage the work God is doing IN and THROUGH this student?

How can I challenge this student to grow?

4

What intentional conversation do I need to have with this student?

What short term and long term goals do I have for this student?

DISCIPLESHIP MAP

1. Check the boxes of words or phrases in both columns that represent or describe your student. If you are unsure or don't know this student in a particular area, then feel free to leave the box empty.

2. When you are finished, look at which of the eight areas (Rescue, Identity, and so on) show a lot of depth—many items checked on the left side and few on the right. Consider how you can encourage or support this student in those areas (an encouragement note, text, or even pointing them to an opportunity where they could continue to grow deeper).

3. Next, decipher which of the eight areas is a struggle for your student, where the warning signs are greatly mounted against the traces of depth. Consider how you might challenge and come alongside your student. A great place to start is with prayer (check out the prayer page for each student) and by adding step-by-step goals or challenges to the Growth Plan (page 48).

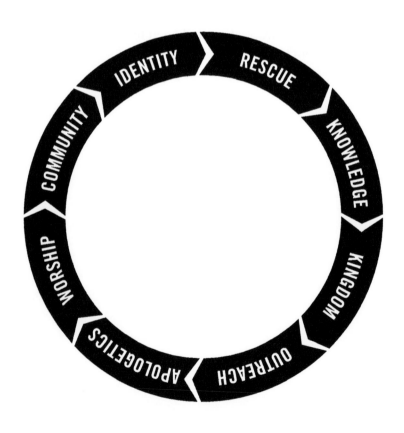

RESCUE: Students who are deeply rooted in their story of being rescued by Christ (salvation and redemption) often show these traces of depth. Students who might not completely grasp this part of discipleship show these warning signs. Check the boxes of words or phrases in both columns that reflect your student's lifestyle.

*For a more complete definition of "Rescue," Scripture verses, as well as some questions to guide a student in their discipleship journey related to this area (and all eight discipleship areas), check out the appendix on page 116.

TRACES OF DEPTH	WARNING SIGNS
❏ passion for evangelism	❏ works-based faith
❏ thankfulness	❏ tries to earn God's love
❏ sacrifices for God and/or others	❏ points fingers
❏ uncompromising	❏ holds onto guilt and shame
❏ lifestyle consistency (same person in all places and circumstances)	❏ holds grudges
	❏ keeps score
❏ confession/repentance is a part of their life	❏ makes excuses
❏ offers forgiveness	❏ acts entitled
❏ shows grace to others and self	❏ blames others often
❏ a realized need for a Savior	❏ takes God's grace for granted
❏ understands consequences of sin	

4

KNOWLEDGE: Students who are deeply rooted in the truth about who God is and their pursuit of knowing him often show these traces of depth. Students who might hold a false sense of God, or haven't pursued knowing God may display these warning signs. (Go deeper on page 118.)

TRACES OF DEPTH	WARNING SIGNS
❏ a growing awe	❏ growing pride
❏ healthy fear of God	❏ acknowledges more than one God
❏ value for God's Word	
❏ knows the God of the Bible	❏ hides from God
❏ humility/self-awareness	❏ foolishness
❏ growing love/desire to know him	❏ lacks value for God's word
❏ worshipful lifestyle	❏ apathy
❏ God is a part of decisions	❏ seeks beyond God
❏ relationship with God exists beyond the church walls	❏ anger at God
❏ reflects wisdom	❏ expects God to have no involvement
	❏ makes him/herself God of their life

IDENTITY: Students who are deeply rooted in their identity as God's children often show some of these traces of depth. Students who struggle to know or live out this identity may display some of these warning signs. (Go deeper on page 120.)

TRACES OF DEPTH	WARNING SIGNS
❏ confidence and self-awareness ❏ using spiritual gifts and wiring/personality for the kingdom ❏ consistent lifestyle (same person in all circumstances) ❏ comfortable in their own skin ❏ affirming of others ❏ likes who they are ❏ embraces growth ❏ accepts criticism ❏ honest ❏ accepts and seeks help	❏ puts others down ❏ identity or worth is determined by environment (performance, teams, group, problems, etc.) ❏ trying to be someone they aren't ❏ fear or insecurity ❏ self-deprecating ❏ consumed with outer appearance ❏ depression/anxiety ❏ works to feed ego or people pleaser ❏ social media identity doesn't match reality ❏ me against the world mentality

KINGDOM: Students who are deeply rooted in their understanding of God's kingdom and who are living from a kingdom perspective often show some of these traces of depth. Students who struggle to embrace this perspective and are wrestling with a worldly or cultural perspective may display some of these warning signs.
(Go deeper on page 122.)

TRACES OF DEPTH	WARNING SIGNS
❏ inspired to serve ❏ embracing the last and least ❏ pushes their comfort zone ❏ willing to sacrifice ❏ appreciation for current circumstances ❏ welcoming and inclusive of others ❏ selfless ❏ has a long-term perspective ❏ knows the King ❏ regularly gives without payment (time, money, attention, resources, respect)	❏ driven by materialism ❏ rarely steps outside of comfort zone ❏ one-upmanship ❏ selfish ❏ lives in the moment ❏ sees themselves as king of their life ❏ reckless living ❏ rarely sees ways to serve others ❏ has many "idols" before God ❏ easily overwhelmed by short-term obstacles

4

OUTREACH: Students who are deeply rooted in their desire and ability to reach the lost show some of these traces of depth. Students who struggle to reach out to the lost may display some of these warning signs. (Go deeper on page 124.)

TRACES OF DEPTH	WARNING SIGNS
❏ inspired to serve ❏ seeks out the lost ❏ willing to share their faith story ❏ burden for the lost ❏ uses current situations as outreach (where and who they already are) ❏ gives sacrificially (time, money, gifts, etc.) ❏ deep value for others (beyond friends) ❏ courageously shares God's truth ❏ has positive influence on the lost ❏ desire for justice in the world	❏ selfish ❏ uses people ❏ does things that devalue people ❏ afraid to talk about spiritual things ❏ patronizing/mocking ❏ makes excuses for not reaching out ❏ fear of judgment ❏ unsure of spiritual truth ❏ apathetic ❏ easily influenced by the lost

4

WORSHIP: Students who are deeply rooted in a lifestyle of worship show some of these traces of depth. Students who struggle to worship or show adoration may display some of these warning signs. (Go deeper on page 126.)

TRACES OF DEPTH	WARNING SIGNS
❏ faith is part of their whole life ❏ drawn to worship ❏ gives freely/initiates giving ❏ obedience to God ❏ prayer is a staple and spontaneous ❏ comfortable praying in groups/out loud ❏ thankfulness ❏ desire to imitate Christ/God ❏ worships regardless of circumstance ❏ joyful	❏ many idols (things they value higher than God) ❏ showy worship ❏ takes things for granted ❏ many spiritual highs and lows ❏ feeling-based faith/worship ❏ overly critical of worship styles ❏ shallow prayer life ❏ only worships by singing ❏ worship is compartmentalized to church ❏ sacrifices begrudgingly

APOLOGETICS: Students who are deeply rooted in the truths that sustain their faith show some of these traces of depth. Students who struggle to know and own the truth of their faith may show some of these warning signs. (Go deeper on page 128.)

TRACES OF DEPTH	WARNING SIGNS
❏ balances knowing God and knowing about God ❏ able to communicate faith story ❏ has spiritual mentors ❏ honest (especially about doubt or unknowns) ❏ humble ❏ willingness to learn/teachable ❏ has a recognizable faith ❏ lovingly holds that Christ is the only way ❏ speaks truth in love ❏ high value for the Bible	❏ combative/argumentative ❏ unteachable ❏ believes all opinions on God are true ❏ thinks they have it all figured out ❏ is okay with many higher powers as true ❏ disregards the Bible ❏ derailed by doubt ❏ cannot articulate their faith ❏ beliefs are easily swayed ❏ lacks spiritual mentoring

COMMUNITY: Students who are deeply rooted in their connection with the community of Christ show some of these traces of depth. Students who struggle to be a part of Christian community may display some of these warning signs. (Go deeper on page 130.)

TRACES OF DEPTH	WARNING SIGNS
❏ has many kinds of relationships (mentor, accountability, mentee, outreach) ❏ peacemaker ❏ encourager ❏ submits to spiritual authority ❏ inclusive/welcoming ❏ promotes unity in the church/youth group ❏ understands their role to minister to the world ❏ authentic living—represents the church in or outside of the building ❏ knows/uses spiritual gifts ❏ serving in the church	❏ isolation ❏ holding grudges ❏ avoiding ❏ gossip ❏ divisive ❏ exclusive ❏ inconsistent lifestyle/attitude and actions ❏ constant critic ❏ parasitic ❏ expecting church to serve them

4

Prayer:

Answers to prayer:

Student Name

[   ]

And anyone who **does not carry
his cross** and follow me CANNOT
BE MY DISCIPLE. **Luke 14:27**

5

Student Profile

Name:

Family life:

Activities:

Passionate about:

Burdened by:

Influenced by:

Testimony:

Spends free time:

5

Growth Plan

	PERSONAL GROWTH: How is God working **IN** this student?	MINISTRY GROWTH: How is God working **THROUGH** this student?
Family		
Peers		
Spiritual Gifts & Wiring		
Leadership		

5

Growth Plan

GROWTH AND GOALS: consider these questions for your student

How can I encourage the work God is doing IN and THROUGH this student?

How can I challenge this student to grow?

5

What intentional conversation do I need to have with this student?

What short term and long term goals do I have for this student?

DISCIPLESHIP MAP

1. Check the boxes of words or phrases in both columns that represent or describe your student. If you are unsure or don't know this student in a particular area, then feel free to leave the box empty.
2. When you are finished, look at which of the eight areas (Rescue, Identity, and so on) show a lot of depth—many items checked on the left side and few on the right. Consider how you can encourage or support this student in those areas (an encouragement note, text, or even pointing them to an opportunity where they could continue to grow deeper).
3. Next, decipher which of the eight areas is a struggle for your student, where the warning signs are greatly mounted against the traces of depth. Consider how you might challenge and come alongside your student. A great place to start is with prayer (check out the prayer page for each student) and by adding step-by-step goals or challenges to the Growth Plan (page 58).

5

RESCUE: Students who are deeply rooted in their story of being rescued by Christ (salvation and redemption) often show these traces of depth. Students who might not completely grasp this part of discipleship show these warning signs. Check the boxes of words or phrases in both columns that reflect your student's lifestyle.

*For a more complete definition of "Rescue," Scripture verses, as well as some questions to guide a student in their discipleship journey related to this area (and all eight discipleship areas), check out the appendix on page 116.

TRACES OF DEPTH	WARNING SIGNS
❑ passion for evangelism	❑ works-based faith
❑ thankfulness	❑ tries to earn God's love
❑ sacrifices for God and/or others	❑ points fingers
❑ uncompromising	❑ holds onto guilt and shame
❑ lifestyle consistency (same person in all places and circumstances)	❑ holds grudges
	❑ keeps score
❑ confession/repentance is a part of their life	❑ makes excuses
❑ offers forgiveness	❑ acts entitled
❑ shows grace to others and self	❑ blames others often
❑ a realized need for a Savior	❑ takes God's grace for granted
❑ understands consequences of sin	

KNOWLEDGE: Students who are deeply rooted in the truth about who God is and their pursuit of knowing him often show these traces of depth. Students who might hold a false sense of God, or haven't pursued knowing God may display these warning signs. (Go deeper on page 118.)

TRACES OF DEPTH	WARNING SIGNS
❑ a growing awe	❑ growing pride
❑ healthy fear of God	❑ acknowledges more than one God
❑ value for God's Word	❑ hides from God
❑ knows the God of the Bible	❑ foolishness
❑ humility/self-awareness	❑ lacks value for God's word
❑ growing love/desire to know him	❑ apathy
❑ worshipful lifestyle	❑ seeks beyond God
❑ God is a part of decisions	❑ anger at God
❑ relationship with God exists beyond the church walls	❑ expects God to have no involvement
❑ reflects wisdom	❑ makes him/herself God of their life

5

IDENTITY: Students who are deeply rooted in their identity as God's children often show some of these traces of depth. Students who struggle to know or live out this identity may display some of these warning signs. (Go deeper on page 120.)

TRACES OF DEPTH	WARNING SIGNS
❏ confidence and self-awareness ❏ using spiritual gifts and wiring/personality for the kingdom ❏ consistent lifestyle (same person in all circumstances) ❏ comfortable in their own skin ❏ affirming of others ❏ likes who they are ❏ embraces growth ❏ accepts criticism ❏ honest ❏ accepts and seeks help	❏ puts others down ❏ identity or worth is determined by environment (performance, teams, groups, problems, etc.) ❏ trying to be someone they aren't ❏ fear or insecurity ❏ self-deprecating ❏ consumed with outer appearance ❏ depression/anxiety ❏ works to feed ego or people pleaser ❏ social media identity doesn't match reality ❏ me against the world mentality

KINGDOM: Students who are deeply rooted in their understanding of God's kingdom and who are living from a kingdom perspective often show some of these traces of depth. Students who struggle to embrace this perspective and are wrestling with a worldly or cultural perspective may display some of these warning signs. (Go deeper on page 122.)

TRACES OF DEPTH	WARNING SIGNS
❏ inspired to serve ❏ embracing the last and least ❏ pushes their comfort zone ❏ willing to sacrifice ❏ appreciation for current circumstances ❏ welcoming and inclusive of others ❏ selfless ❏ has a long-term perspective ❏ knows the King ❏ regularly gives without payment (time, money, attention, resources, respect)	❏ driven by materialism ❏ rarely steps outside of comfort zone ❏ one-upmanship ❏ selfish ❏ lives in the moment ❏ sees themselves as king of their life ❏ reckless living ❏ rarely sees ways to serve others ❏ has many "idols" before God ❏ easily overwhelmed by short-term obstacles

OUTREACH: Students who are deeply rooted in their desire and ability to reach the lost show some of these traces of depth. Students who struggle to reach out to the lost may display some of these warning signs. (Go deeper on page 124.)

TRACES OF DEPTH	WARNING SIGNS
❏ inspired to serve ❏ seeks out the lost ❏ willing to share their faith story ❏ burden for the lost ❏ uses current situations as outreach (where and who they already are) ❏ gives sacrificially (time, money, gifts, etc.) ❏ deep value for others (beyond friends) ❏ courageously shares God's truth ❏ has positive influence on the lost ❏ desire for justice in the world	❏ selfish ❏ uses people ❏ does things that devalue people ❏ afraid to talk about spiritual things ❏ patronizing/mocking ❏ makes excuses for not reaching out ❏ fear of judgment ❏ unsure of spiritual truth ❏ apathetic ❏ easily influenced by the lost

5

WORSHIP: Students who are deeply rooted in a lifestyle of worship show some of these traces of depth. Students who struggle to worship or show adoration may display some of these warning signs. (Go deeper on page 126.)

TRACES OF DEPTH	WARNING SIGNS
❏ faith is part of their whole life ❏ drawn to worship ❏ gives freely/initiates giving ❏ obedience to God ❏ prayer is a staple and spontaneous ❏ comfortable praying in groups/out loud ❏ thankfulness ❏ desire to imitate Christ/God ❏ worships regardless of circumstance ❏ joyful	❏ many idols (things they value higher than God) ❏ showy worship ❏ takes things for granted ❏ many spiritual highs and lows ❏ feeling-based faith/worship ❏ overly critical of worship styles ❏ shallow prayer life ❏ only worships by singing ❏ worship is compartmentalized to church ❏ sacrifices begrudgingly

APOLOGETICS: Students who are deeply rooted in the truths that sustain their faith show some of these traces of depth. Students who struggle to know and own the truth of their faith may show some of these warning signs. (Go deeper on page 128.)

TRACES OF DEPTH	WARNING SIGNS
❏ balances knowing God and knowing about God ❏ able to communicate faith story ❏ has spiritual mentors ❏ honest (especially about doubt or unknowns) ❏ humble ❏ willingness to learn/teachable ❏ has a recognizable faith ❏ lovingly holds that Christ is the only way ❏ speaks truth in love ❏ high value for the Bible	❏ combative/argumentative ❏ unteachable ❏ believes all opinions on God are true ❏ thinks they have it all figured out ❏ is okay with many higher powers as true ❏ disregards the Bible ❏ derailed by doubt ❏ cannot articulate their faith ❏ beliefs are easily swayed ❏ lacks spiritual mentoring

COMMUNITY: Students who are deeply rooted in their connection with the community of Christ show some of these traces of depth. Students who struggle to be a part of Christian community may display some of these warning signs. (Go deeper on page 130.)

TRACES OF DEPTH	WARNING SIGNS
❏ has many kinds of relationships (mentor, accountability, mentee, outreach) ❏ peacemaker ❏ encourager ❏ submits to spiritual authority ❏ inclusive/welcoming ❏ promotes unity in the church/youth group ❏ understands their role to minister to the world ❏ authentic living—represents the church in or outside of the building ❏ knows/uses spiritual gifts ❏ serving in the church	❏ isolation ❏ holding grudges ❏ avoiding ❏ gossip ❏ divisive ❏ exclusive ❏ inconsistent lifestyle/attitude and actions ❏ constant critic ❏ parasitic ❏ expecting church to serve them

Prayer:

Answers to prayer:

Student Name

[   ]

HE IS NO FOOL who **gives what he cannot
keep** to GAIN WHAT HE CANNOT LOSE.
—Jim Elliot *(Shadow of the Almighty)*

6

Student Profile

Name:

Family life:

Activities:

Passionate about:

Burdened by:

Influenced by:

Testimony:

Spends free time:

Growth Plan

	PERSONAL GROWTH: How is God working **IN** this student?	MINISTRY GROWTH: How is God working **THROUGH** this student?
Family		
Peers		
Spiritual Gifts & Wiring		
Leadership		

6

Growth Plan

GROWTH AND GOALS: consider these questions for your student

How can I encourage the work God is doing IN and
THROUGH this student?

How can I challenge this student to grow?

What intentional conversation do I need to have
with this student?

6

What short term and long term goals do I have for
this student?

DISCIPLESHIP MAP

1. Check the boxes of words or phrases in both columns that represent or describe your student. If you are unsure or don't know this student in a particular area, then feel free to leave the box empty.
2. When you are finished, look at which of the eight areas (Rescue, Identity, and so on) show a lot of depth—many items checked on the left side and few on the right. Consider how you can encourage or support this student in those areas (an encouragement note, text, or even pointing them to an opportunity where they could continue to grow deeper).
3. Next, decipher which of the eight areas is a struggle for your student, where the warning signs are greatly mounted against the traces of depth. Consider how you might challenge and come alongside your student. A great place to start is with prayer (check out the prayer page for each student) and by adding step-by-step goals or challenges to the Growth Plan (page 68).

RESCUE: Students who are deeply rooted in their story of being rescued by Christ (salvation and redemption) often show these traces of depth. Students who might not completely grasp this part of discipleship show these warning signs. Check the boxes of words or phrases in both columns that reflect your student's lifestyle.

*For a more complete definition of "Rescue," Scripture verses, as well as some questions to guide a student in their discipleship journey related to this area (and all eight discipleship areas), check out the appendix on page 116.

TRACES OF DEPTH	WARNING SIGNS
❏ passion for evangelism	❏ works-based faith
❏ thankfulness	❏ tries to earn God's love
❏ sacrifices for God and/or others	❏ points fingers
❏ uncompromising	❏ holds onto guilt and shame
❏ lifestyle consistency (same person in all places and circumstances)	❏ holds grudges
	❏ keeps score
❏ confession/repentance is a part of their life	❏ makes excuses
❏ offers forgiveness	❏ acts entitled
❏ shows grace to others and self	❏ blames others often
❏ a realized need for a Savior	❏ takes God's grace for granted
❏ understands consequences of sin	

KNOWLEDGE: Students who are deeply rooted in the truth about who God is and their pursuit of knowing him often show these traces of depth. Students who might hold a false sense of God, or haven't pursued knowing God may display these warning signs. (Go deeper on page 118.)

6

TRACES OF DEPTH	WARNING SIGNS
❏ a growing awe	❏ growing pride
❏ healthy fear of God	❏ acknowledges more than one God
❏ value for God's Word	
❏ knows the God of the Bible	❏ hides from God
❏ humility/self-awareness	❏ foolishness
❏ growing love/desire to know him	❏ lacks value for God's word
❏ worshipful lifestyle	❏ apathy
❏ God is a part of decisions	❏ seeks beyond God
❏ relationship with God exists beyond the church walls	❏ anger at God
❏ reflects wisdom	❏ expects God to have no involvement
	❏ makes him/herself God of their life

IDENTITY: Students who are deeply rooted in their identity as God's children often show some of these traces of depth. Students who struggle to know or live out this identity may display some of these warning signs. (Go deeper on page 120.)

TRACES OF DEPTH	WARNING SIGNS
❏ confidence and self-awareness ❏ using spiritual gifts and wiring/personality for the kingdom ❏ consistent lifestyle (same person in all circumstances) ❏ comfortable in their own skin ❏ affirming of others ❏ likes who they are ❏ embraces growth ❏ accepts criticism ❏ honest ❏ accepts and seeks help	❏ puts others down ❏ identity or worth is determined by environment (performance, teams, groups, problems, etc.) ❏ trying to be someone they aren't ❏ fear or insecurity ❏ self-deprecating ❏ consumed with outer appearance ❏ depression/anxiety ❏ works to feed ego or people pleaser ❏ social media identity doesn't match reality ❏ me against the world mentality

KINGDOM: Students who are deeply rooted in their understanding of God's kingdom and who are living from a kingdom perspective often show some of these traces of depth. Students who struggle to embrace this perspective and are wrestling with a worldly or cultural perspective may display some of these warning signs.
(Go deeper on page 122.)

TRACES OF DEPTH	WARNING SIGNS
❏ inspired to serve ❏ embracing the last and least ❏ pushes their comfort zone ❏ willing to sacrifice ❏ appreciation for current circumstances ❏ welcoming and inclusive of others ❏ selfless ❏ has a long-term perspective ❏ knows the King ❏ regularly gives without payment (time, money, attention, resources, respect)	❏ driven by materialism ❏ rarely steps outside of comfort zone ❏ one-upmanship ❏ selfish ❏ lives in the moment ❏ sees themselves as king of their life ❏ reckless living ❏ rarely sees ways to serve others ❏ has many "idols" before God ❏ easily overwhelmed by short-term obstacles

OUTREACH: Students who are deeply rooted in their desire and ability to reach the lost show some of these traces of depth. Students who struggle to reach out to the lost may display some of these warning signs. (Go deeper on page 124.)

TRACES OF DEPTH	WARNING SIGNS
❑ inspired to serve ❑ seeks out the lost ❑ willing to share their faith story ❑ burden for the lost ❑ uses current situations as outreach (where and who they already are) ❑ gives sacrificially (time, money, gifts, etc.) ❑ deep value for others (beyond friends) ❑ courageously shares God's truth ❑ has positive influence on the lost ❑ desire for justice in the world	❑ selfish ❑ uses people ❑ does things that devalue people ❑ afraid to talk about spiritual things ❑ patronizing/mocking ❑ makes excuses for not reaching out ❑ fear of judgment ❑ unsure of spiritual truth ❑ apathetic ❑ easily influenced by the lost

WORSHIP: Students who are deeply rooted in a lifestyle of worship show some of these traces of depth. Students who struggle to worship or show adoration may display some of these warning signs. (Go deeper on page 126.)

TRACES OF DEPTH	WARNING SIGNS
❑ faith is part of their whole life ❑ drawn to worship ❑ gives freely/initiates giving ❑ obedience to God ❑ prayer is a staple and spontaneous ❑ comfortable praying in groups/out loud ❑ thankfulness ❑ desire to imitate Christ/God ❑ worships regardless of circumstance ❑ joyful	❑ many idols (things they value higher than God) ❑ showy worship ❑ takes things for granted ❑ many spiritual highs and lows ❑ feeling-based faith/worship ❑ overly critical of worship styles ❑ shallow prayer life ❑ only worships by singing ❑ worship is compartmentalized to church ❑ sacrifices begrudgingly

6

APOLOGETICS:
Students who are deeply rooted in the truths that sustain their faith show some of these traces of depth. Students who struggle to know and own the truth of their faith may show some of these warning signs. (Go deeper on page 128.)

TRACES OF DEPTH	WARNING SIGNS
❏ balances knowing God and knowing about God	❏ combative/argumentative
❏ able to communicate faith story	❏ unteachable
❏ has spiritual mentors	❏ believes all opinions on God are true
❏ honest (especially about doubt or unknowns)	❏ thinks they have it all figured out
❏ humble	❏ is okay with many higher powers as true
❏ willingness to learn/teachable	❏ disregards the Bible
❏ has a recognizable faith	❏ derailed by doubt
❏ lovingly holds that Christ is the only way	❏ cannot articulate their faith
❏ speaks truth in love	❏ beliefs are easily swayed
❏ high value for the Bible	❏ lacks spiritual mentoring

COMMUNITY:
Students who are deeply rooted in their connection with the community of Christ show some of these traces of depth. Students who struggle to be a part of Christian community may display some of these warning signs. (Go deeper on page 130.)

TRACES OF DEPTH	WARNING SIGNS
❏ has many kinds of relationships (mentor, accountability, mentee, outreach)	❏ isolation
❏ peacemaker	❏ holding grudges
❏ encourager	❏ avoiding
❏ submits to spiritual authority	❏ gossip
❏ inclusive/welcoming	❏ divisive
❏ promotes unity in the church/youth group	❏ exclusive
❏ understands their role to minister to the world	❏ inconsistent lifestyle/attitude and actions
❏ authentic living—represents the church in or outside of the building	❏ constant critic
❏ knows/uses spiritual gifts	❏ parasitic
❏ serving in the church	❏ expecting church to serve them

Prayer:

Answers to prayer:

6

Student Name

[   ]

AND I PRAY THAT YOU, being rooted and established in love, may have power, together with the saints, **to grasp how wide and long and high and deep is the love of Christ,** and to know this love that surpasses knowledge—that you may be FILLED TO THE MEASURE OF ALL THE FULLNESS OF GOD.
Ephesians 3:17b–19

7

Student Profile

Name: _____

Family life: _____

_____

Activities: _____

_____

Passionate about: _____

_____

Burdened by: _____

_____

Influenced by: _____

_____

Testimony: _____

_____

Spends free time: _____

Growth Plan

	PERSONAL GROWTH: How is God working **IN** this student?	MINISTRY GROWTH: How is God working **THROUGH** this student?
Family		
Peers		
Spiritual Gifts & Wiring		
Leadership		

7

Growth Plan

GROWTH AND GOALS: consider these questions for your student

How can I encourage the work God is doing IN and THROUGH this student?

How can I challenge this student to grow?

What intentional conversation do I need to have with this student?

What short term and long term goals do I have for this student?

7

DISCIPLESHIP MAP

1. Check the boxes of words or phrases in both columns that represent or describe your student. If you are unsure or don't know this student in a particular area, then feel free to leave the box empty.
2. When you are finished, look at which of the eight areas (Rescue, Identity, and so on) show a lot of depth—many items checked on the left side and few on the right. Consider how you can encourage or support this student in those areas (an encouragement note, text, or even pointing them to an opportunity where they could continue to grow deeper).
3. Next, decipher which of the eight areas is a struggle for your student, where the warning signs are greatly mounted against the traces of depth. Consider how you might challenge and come alongside your student. A great place to start is with prayer (check out the prayer page for each student) and by adding step-by-step goals or challenges to the Growth Plan (page 78).

RESCUE: Students who are deeply rooted in their story of being rescued by Christ (salvation and redemption) often show these traces of depth. Students who might not completely grasp this part of discipleship show these warning signs. Check the boxes of words or phrases in both columns that reflect your student's lifestyle.

*For a more complete definition of "Rescue," Scripture verses, as well as some questions to guide a student in their discipleship journey related to this area (and all eight discipleship areas), check out the appendix on page 116.

TRACES OF DEPTH	WARNING SIGNS
❏ passion for evangelism	❏ works-based faith
❏ thankfulness	❏ tries to earn God's love
❏ sacrifices for God and/or others	❏ points fingers
❏ uncompromising	❏ holds onto guilt and shame
❏ lifestyle consistency (same person in all places and circumstances)	❏ holds grudges
	❏ keeps score
❏ confession/repentance is a part of their life	❏ makes excuses
❏ offers forgiveness	❏ acts entitled
❏ shows grace to others and self	❏ blames others often
❏ a realized need for a Savior	❏ takes God's grace for granted
❏ understands consequences of sin	

KNOWLEDGE: Students who are deeply rooted in the truth about who God is and their pursuit of knowing him often show these traces of depth. Students who might hold a false sense of God, or haven't pursued knowing God may display these warning signs. (Go deeper on page 118.)

TRACES OF DEPTH	WARNING SIGNS
❏ a growing awe	❏ growing pride
❏ healthy fear of God	❏ acknowledges more than one God
❏ value for God's Word	
❏ knows the God of the Bible	❏ hides from God
❏ humility/self-awareness	❏ foolishness
❏ growing love/desire to know him	❏ lacks value for God's word
❏ worshipful lifestyle	❏ apathy
❏ God is a part of decisions	❏ seeks beyond God
❏ relationship with God exists beyond the church walls	❏ anger at God
❏ reflects wisdom	❏ expects God to have no involvement
	❏ makes him/herself God of their life

7

IDENTITY:
Students who are deeply rooted in their identity as God's children often show some of these traces of depth. Students who struggle to know or live out this identity may display some of these warning signs. (Go deeper on page 120.)

TRACES OF DEPTH	WARNING SIGNS
❏ confidence and self-awareness ❏ using spiritual gifts and wiring/personality for the kingdom ❏ consistent lifestyle (same person in all circumstances) ❏ comfortable in their own skin ❏ affirming of others ❏ likes who they are ❏ embraces growth ❏ accepts criticism ❏ honest ❏ accepts and seeks help	❏ puts others down ❏ identity or worth is determined by environment (performance, teams, group, problems, etc.) ❏ trying to be someone they aren't ❏ fear or insecurity ❏ self-deprecating ❏ consumed with outer appearance ❏ depression/anxiety ❏ works to feed ego or people pleaser ❏ social media identity doesn't match reality ❏ me against the world mentality

KINGDOM:
Students who are deeply rooted in their understanding of God's kingdom and who are living from a kingdom perspective often show some of these traces of depth. Students who struggle to embrace this perspective and are wrestling with a worldly or cultural perspective may display some of these warning signs.
(Go deeper on page 122.)

TRACES OF DEPTH	WARNING SIGNS
❏ inspired to serve ❏ embracing the last and least ❏ pushes their comfort zone ❏ willing to sacrifice ❏ appreciation for current circumstances ❏ welcoming and inclusive of others ❏ selfless ❏ has a long-term perspective ❏ knows the King ❏ regularly gives without payment (time, money, attention, resources, respect)	❏ driven by materialism ❏ rarely steps outside of comfort zone ❏ one-upmanship ❏ selfish ❏ lives in the moment ❏ sees themselves as king of their life ❏ reckless living ❏ rarely sees ways to serve others ❏ has many "idols" before God ❏ easily overwhelmed by short-term obstacles

OUTREACH: Students who are deeply rooted in their desire and ability to reach the lost show some of these traces of depth. Students who struggle to reach out to the lost may display some of these warning signs. (Go deeper on page 124.)

TRACES OF DEPTH	WARNING SIGNS
❏ inspired to serve ❏ seeks out the lost ❏ willing to share their faith story ❏ burden for the lost ❏ uses current situations as outreach (where and who they already are) ❏ gives sacrificially (time, money, gifts, etc.) ❏ deep value for others (beyond friends) ❏ courageously shares God's truth ❏ has positive influence on the lost ❏ desire for justice in the world	❏ selfish ❏ uses people ❏ does things that devalue people ❏ afraid to talk about spiritual things ❏ patronizing/mocking ❏ makes excuses for not reaching out ❏ fear of judgment ❏ unsure of spiritual truth ❏ apathetic ❏ easily influenced by the lost

WORSHIP: Students who are deeply rooted in a lifestyle of worship show some of these traces of depth. Students who struggle to worship or show adoration may display some of these warning signs. (Go deeper on page 126.)

TRACES OF DEPTH	WARNING SIGNS
❏ faith is part of their whole life ❏ drawn to worship ❏ gives freely/initiates giving ❏ obedience to God ❏ prayer is a staple and spontaneous ❏ comfortable praying in groups/out loud ❏ thankfulness ❏ desire to imitate Christ/God ❏ worships regardless of circumstance ❏ joyful	❏ many idols (things they value higher than God) ❏ showy worship ❏ takes things for granted ❏ many spiritual highs and lows ❏ feeling-based faith/worship ❏ overly critical of worship styles ❏ shallow prayer life ❏ only worships by singing ❏ worship is compartmentalized to church ❏ sacrifices begrudgingly

7

83

APOLOGETICS: Students who are deeply rooted in the truths that sustain their faith show some of these traces of depth. Students who struggle to know and own the truth of their faith may show some of these warning signs. (Go deeper on page 128.)

TRACES OF DEPTH	WARNING SIGNS
❏ balances knowing God and knowing about God ❏ able to communicate faith story ❏ has spiritual mentors ❏ honest (especially about doubt or unknowns) ❏ humble ❏ willingness to learn/teachable ❏ has a recognizable faith ❏ lovingly holds that Christ is the only way ❏ speaks truth in love ❏ high value for the Bible	❏ combative/argumentative ❏ unteachable ❏ believes all opinions on God are true ❏ thinks they have it all figured out ❏ is okay with many higher powers as true ❏ disregards the Bible ❏ derailed by doubt ❏ cannot articulate their faith ❏ beliefs are easily swayed ❏ lacks spiritual mentoring

COMMUNITY: Students who are deeply rooted in their connection with the community of Christ show some of these traces of depth. Students who struggle to be a part of Christian community may display some of these warning signs. (Go deeper on page 130.)

TRACES OF DEPTH	WARNING SIGNS
❏ has many kinds of relationships (mentor, accountability, mentee, outreach) ❏ peacemaker ❏ encourager ❏ submits to spiritual authority ❏ inclusive/welcoming ❏ promotes unity in the church/youth group ❏ understands their role to minister to the world ❏ authentic living—represents the church in or outside of the building ❏ knows/uses spiritual gifts ❏ serving in the church	❏ isolation ❏ holding grudges ❏ avoiding ❏ gossip ❏ divisive ❏ exclusive ❏ inconsistent lifestyle/attitude and actions ❏ constant critic ❏ parasitic ❏ expecting church to serve them

Prayer:

Answers to prayer:

Student Name

[   ]

Going to church **doesn't make you a Christian** any more than going to McDonald's MAKES YOU A HAMBURGER. —Keith Green

(No Compromise: The Life Story of Keith Green)

Student Profile

Name: _____

Family life: _____

_____

Activities: _____

_____

Passionate about: _____

_____

Burdened by: _____

_____

Influenced by: _____

_____

Testimony: _____

8

_____

Spends free time: _____

Growth Plan

	PERSONAL GROWTH: How is God working **IN** this student?	MINISTRY GROWTH: How is God working **THROUGH** this student?
Family		
Peers		
Spiritual Gifts & Wiring		
Leadership		

Growth Plan

GROWTH AND GOALS: consider these questions for your student

How can I encourage the work God is doing IN and
THROUGH this student?

How can I challenge this student to grow?

What intentional conversation do I need to have
with this student?

What short term and long term goals do I have for
this student?

8

DISCIPLESHIP MAP

1. Check the boxes of words or phrases in both columns that represent or describe your student. If you are unsure or don't know this student in a particular area, then feel free to leave the box empty.
2. When you are finished, look at which of the eight areas (Rescue, Identity, and so on) show a lot of depth—many items checked on the left side and few on the right. Consider how you can encourage or support this student in those areas (an encouragement note, text, or even pointing them to an opportunity where they could continue to grow deeper).
3. Next, decipher which of the eight areas is a struggle for your student, where the warning signs are greatly mounted against the traces of depth. Consider how you might challenge and come alongside your student. A great place to start is with prayer (check out the prayer page for each student) and by adding step-by-step goals or challenges to the Growth Plan (page 88).

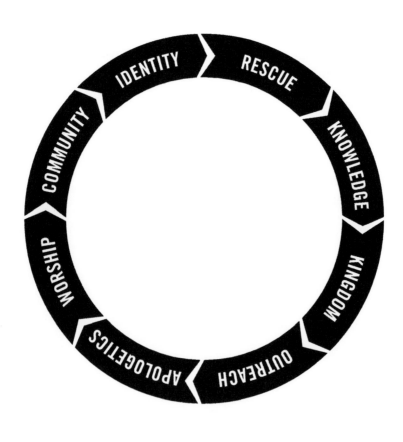

RESCUE: Students who are deeply rooted in their story of being rescued by Christ (salvation and redemption) often show these traces of depth. Students who might not completely grasp this part of discipleship show these warning signs. Check the boxes of words or phrases in both columns that reflect your student's lifestyle.

*For a more complete definition of "Rescue," Scripture verses, as well as some questions to guide a student in their discipleship journey related to this area (and all eight discipleship areas), check out the appendix on page 116.

TRACES OF DEPTH	WARNING SIGNS
❏ passion for evangelism ❏ thankfulness ❏ sacrifices for God and/or others ❏ uncompromising ❏ lifestyle consistency (same person in all places and circumstances) ❏ confession/repentance is a part of their life ❏ offers forgiveness ❏ shows grace to others and self ❏ a realized need for a Savior ❏ understands consequences of sin	❏ works-based faith ❏ tries to earn God's love ❏ points fingers ❏ holds onto guilt and shame ❏ holds grudges ❏ keeps score ❏ makes excuses ❏ acts entitled ❏ blames others often ❏ takes God's grace for granted

KNOWLEDGE: Students who are deeply rooted in the truth about who God is and their pursuit of knowing him often show these traces of depth. Students who might hold a false sense of God, or haven't pursued knowing God may display these warning signs. (Go deeper on page 118.)

TRACES OF DEPTH	WARNING SIGNS
❏ a growing awe ❏ healthy fear of God ❏ value for God's Word ❏ knows the God of the Bible ❏ humility/self-awareness ❏ growing love/desire to know him ❏ worshipful lifestyle ❏ God is a part of decisions ❏ relationship with God exists beyond the church walls ❏ reflects wisdom	❏ growing pride ❏ acknowledges more than one God ❏ hides from God ❏ foolishness ❏ lacks value for God's word ❏ apathy ❏ seeks beyond God ❏ anger at God ❏ expects God to have no involvement ❏ makes him/herself God of their life

8

IDENTITY: Students who are deeply rooted in their identity as God's children often show some of these traces of depth. Students who struggle to know or live out this identity may display some of these warning signs. (Go deeper on page 120.)

TRACES OF DEPTH	WARNING SIGNS
❏ confidence and self-awareness ❏ using spiritual gifts and wiring/personality for the kingdom ❏ consistent lifestyle (same person in all circumstances) ❏ comfortable in their own skin ❏ affirming of others ❏ likes who they are ❏ embraces growth ❏ accepts criticism ❏ honest ❏ accepts and seeks help	❏ puts others down ❏ identity or worth is determined by environment (performance, teams, groups, problems, etc.) ❏ trying to be someone they aren't ❏ fear or insecurity ❏ self-deprecating ❏ consumed with outer appearance ❏ depression/anxiety ❏ works to feed ego or people pleaser ❏ social media identity doesn't match reality ❏ me against the world mentality

KINGDOM: Students who are deeply rooted in their understanding of God's kingdom and who are living from a kingdom perspective often show some of these traces of depth. Students who struggle to embrace this perspective and are wrestling with a worldly or cultural perspective may display some of these warning signs. (Go deeper on page 122.)

TRACES OF DEPTH	WARNING SIGNS
❏ inspired to serve ❏ embracing the last and least ❏ pushes their comfort zone ❏ willing to sacrifice ❏ appreciation for current circumstances ❏ welcoming and inclusive of others ❏ selfless ❏ has a long-term perspective ❏ knows the King ❏ regularly gives without payment (time, money, attention, resources, respect)	❏ driven by materialism ❏ rarely steps outside of comfort zone ❏ one-upmanship ❏ selfish ❏ lives in the moment ❏ sees themselves as king of their life ❏ reckless living ❏ rarely sees ways to serve others ❏ has many "idols" before God ❏ easily overwhelmed by short-term obstacles

8

OUTREACH: Students who are deeply rooted in their desire and ability to reach the lost show some of these traces of depth. Students who struggle to reach out to the lost may display some of these warning signs. (Go deeper on page 124.)

TRACES OF DEPTH	WARNING SIGNS
❑ inspired to serve ❑ seeks out the lost ❑ willing to share their faith story ❑ burden for the lost ❑ uses current situations as outreach (where and who they already are) ❑ gives sacrificially (time, money, gifts, etc.) ❑ deep value for others (beyond friends) ❑ courageously shares God's truth ❑ has positive influence on the lost ❑ desire for justice in the world	❑ selfish ❑ uses people ❑ does things that devalue people ❑ afraid to talk about spiritual things ❑ patronizing/mocking ❑ makes excuses for not reaching out ❑ fear of judgment ❑ unsure of spiritual truth ❑ apathetic ❑ easily influenced by the lost

WORSHIP: Students who are deeply rooted in a lifestyle of worship show some of these traces of depth. Students who struggle to worship or show adoration may display some of these warning signs. (Go deeper on page 126.)

TRACES OF DEPTH	WARNING SIGNS
❑ faith is part of their whole life ❑ drawn to worship ❑ gives freely/initiates giving ❑ obedience to God ❑ prayer is a staple and spontaneous ❑ comfortable praying in groups/out loud ❑ thankfulness ❑ desire to imitate Christ/God ❑ worships regardless of circumstance ❑ joyful	❑ many idols (things they value higher than God) ❑ showy worship ❑ takes things for granted ❑ many spiritual highs and lows ❑ feeling-based faith/worship ❑ overly critical of worship styles ❑ shallow prayer life ❑ only worships by singing ❑ worship is compartmentalized to church ❑ sacrifices begrudgingly

8

APOLOGETICS: Students who are deeply rooted in the truths that sustain their faith show some of these traces of depth. Students who struggle to know and own the truth of their faith may show some of these warning signs. (Go deeper on page 128.)

TRACES OF DEPTH	WARNING SIGNS
❏ balances knowing God and knowing about God	❏ combative/argumentative
❏ able to communicate faith story	❏ unteachable
❏ has spiritual mentors	❏ believes all opinions on God are true
❏ honest (especially about doubt or unknowns)	❏ thinks they have it all figured out
❏ humble	❏ is okay with many higher powers as true
❏ willingness to learn/teachable	❏ disregards the Bible
❏ has a recognizable faith	❏ derailed by doubt
❏ lovingly holds that Christ is the only way	❏ cannot articulate their faith
❏ speaks truth in love	❏ beliefs are easily swayed
❏ high value for the Bible	❏ lacks spiritual mentoring

COMMUNITY: Students who are deeply rooted in their connection with the community of Christ show some of these traces of depth. Students who struggle to be a part of Christian community may display some of these warning signs. (Go deeper on page 130.)

TRACES OF DEPTH	WARNING SIGNS
❏ has many kinds of relationships (mentor, accountability, mentee, outreach)	❏ isolation
❏ peacemaker	❏ holding grudges
❏ encourager	❏ avoiding
❏ submits to spiritual authority	❏ gossip
❏ inclusive/welcoming	❏ divisive
❏ promotes unity in the church/youth group	❏ exclusive
❏ understands their role to minister to the world	❏ inconsistent lifestyle/attitude and actions
❏ authentic living—represents the church in or outside of the building	❏ constant critic
❏ knows/uses spiritual gifts	❏ parasitic
❏ serving in the church	❏ expecting church to serve them

8

Prayer:

Answers to prayer:

8

Student Name

[   ]

AS A PRISONER FOR THE LORD, then,
I urge you to **live a life worthy** of the
calling you have received. **Ephesians 4:1**

9

Student Profile

Name: _____

Family life: _____

_____

Activities: _____

_____

Passionate about: _____

_____

Burdened by: _____

_____

Influenced by: _____

_____

Testimony: _____

_____

Spends free time: _____

9

Growth Plan

	PERSONAL GROWTH: How is God working **IN** this student?	MINISTRY GROWTH: How is God working **THROUGH** this student?
Family		
Peers		
Spiritual Gifts & Wiring		
Leadership		

9

Growth Plan

GROWTH AND GOALS: consider these questions for your student

How can I encourage the work God is doing IN and THROUGH this student?

How can I challenge this student to grow?

What intentional conversation do I need to have with this student?

What short term and long term goals do I have for this student?

9

DISCIPLESHIP MAP

1. Check the boxes of words or phrases in both columns that represent or describe your student. If you are unsure or don't know this student in a particular area, then feel free to leave the box empty.
2. When you are finished, look at which of the eight areas (Rescue, Identity, and so on) show a lot of depth—many items checked on the left side and few on the right. Consider how you can encourage or support this student in those areas (an encouragement note, text, or even pointing them to an opportunity where they could continue to grow deeper).
3. Next, decipher which of the eight areas is a struggle for your student, where the warning signs are greatly mounted against the traces of depth. Consider how you might challenge and come alongside your student. A great place to start is with prayer (check out the prayer page for each student) and by adding step-by-step goals or challenges to the Growth Plan (page 98).

RESCUE: Students who are deeply rooted in their story of being rescued by Christ (salvation and redemption) often show these traces of depth. Students who might not completely grasp this part of discipleship show these warning signs. Check the boxes of words or phrases in both columns that reflect your student's lifestyle.

*For a more complete definition of "Rescue," Scripture verses, as well as some questions to guide a student in their discipleship journey related to this area (and all eight discipleship areas), check out the appendix on page 116.

TRACES OF DEPTH	WARNING SIGNS
❏ passion for evangelism	❏ works-based faith
❏ thankfulness	❏ tries to earn God's love
❏ sacrifices for God and/or others	❏ points fingers
❏ uncompromising	❏ holds onto guilt and shame
❏ lifestyle consistency (same person in all places and circumstances)	❏ holds grudges
❏ confession/repentance is a part of their life	❏ keeps score
❏ offers forgiveness	❏ makes excuses
❏ shows grace to others and self	❏ acts entitled
❏ a realized need for a Savior	❏ blames others often
❏ understands consequences of sin	❏ takes God's grace for granted

KNOWLEDGE: Students who are deeply rooted in the truth about who God is and their pursuit of knowing him often show these traces of depth. Students who might hold a false sense of God, or haven't pursued knowing God may display these warning signs. (Go deeper on page 118.)

TRACES OF DEPTH	WARNING SIGNS
❏ a growing awe	❏ growing pride
❏ healthy fear of God	❏ acknowledges more than one God
❏ value for God's Word	
❏ knows the God of the Bible	❏ hides from God
❏ humility/self-awareness	❏ foolishness
❏ growing love/desire to know him	❏ lacks value for God's word
❏ worshipful lifestyle	❏ apathy
❏ God is a part of decisions	❏ seeks beyond God
❏ relationship with God exists beyond the church walls	❏ anger at God
❏ reflects wisdom	❏ expects God to have no involvement
	❏ makes him/herself God of their life

9

IDENTITY:
Students who are deeply rooted in their identity as God's children often show some of these traces of depth. Students who struggle to know or live out this identity may display some of these warning signs. (Go deeper on page 120.)

TRACES OF DEPTH	WARNING SIGNS
❏ confidence and self-awareness ❏ using spiritual gifts and wiring/personality for the kingdom ❏ consistent lifestyle (same person in all circumstances) ❏ comfortable in their own skin ❏ affirming of others ❏ likes who they are ❏ embraces growth ❏ accepts criticism ❏ honest ❏ accepts and seeks help	❏ puts others down ❏ identity or worth is determined by environment (performance, teams, groups, problems, etc.) ❏ trying to be someone they aren't ❏ fear or insecurity ❏ self-deprecating ❏ consumed with outer appearance ❏ depression/anxiety ❏ works to feed ego or people pleaser ❏ social media identity doesn't match reality ❏ me against the world mentality

KINGDOM:
Students who are deeply rooted in their understanding of God's kingdom and who are living from a kingdom perspective often show some of these traces of depth. Students who struggle to embrace this perspective and are wrestling with a worldly or cultural perspective may display some of these warning signs.
(Go deeper on page 122.)

TRACES OF DEPTH	WARNING SIGNS
❏ inspired to serve ❏ embracing the last and least ❏ pushes their comfort zone ❏ willing to sacrifice ❏ appreciation for current circumstances ❏ welcoming and inclusive of others ❏ selfless ❏ has a long-term perspective ❏ knows the King ❏ regularly gives without payment (time, money, attention, resources, respect)	❏ driven by materialism ❏ rarely steps outside of comfort zone ❏ one-upmanship ❏ selfish ❏ lives in the moment ❏ sees themselves as king of their life ❏ reckless living ❏ rarely sees ways to serve others ❏ has many "idols" before God ❏ easily overwhelmed by short-term obstacles

OUTREACH: Students who are deeply rooted in their desire and ability to reach the lost show some of these traces of depth. Students who struggle to reach out to the lost may display some of these warning signs. (Go deeper on page 124.)

TRACES OF DEPTH	WARNING SIGNS
❏ inspired to serve ❏ seeks out the lost ❏ willing to share their faith story ❏ burden for the lost ❏ uses current situations as outreach (where and who they already are) ❏ gives sacrificially (time, money, gifts, etc.) ❏ deep value for others (beyond friends) ❏ courageously shares God's truth ❏ has positive influence on the lost ❏ desire for justice in the world	❏ selfish ❏ uses people ❏ does things that devalue people ❏ afraid to talk about spiritual things ❏ patronizing/mocking ❏ makes excuses for not reaching out ❏ fear of judgment ❏ unsure of spiritual truth ❏ apathetic ❏ easily influenced by the lost

WORSHIP: Students who are deeply rooted in a lifestyle of worship show some of these traces of depth. Students who struggle to worship or show adoration may display some of these warning signs. (Go deeper on page 126.)

TRACES OF DEPTH	WARNING SIGNS
❏ faith is part of their whole life ❏ drawn to worship ❏ gives freely/initiates giving ❏ obedience to God ❏ prayer is a staple and spontaneous ❏ comfortable praying in groups/out loud ❏ thankfulness ❏ desire to imitate Christ/God ❏ worships regardless of circumstance ❏ joyful	❏ many idols (things they value higher than God) ❏ showy worship ❏ takes things for granted ❏ many spiritual highs and lows ❏ feeling-based faith/worship ❏ overly critical of worship styles ❏ shallow prayer life ❏ only worships by singing ❏ worship is compartmentalized to church ❏ sacrifices begrudgingly

9

APOLOGETICS: Students who are deeply rooted in the truths that sustain their faith show some of these traces of depth. Students who struggle to know and own the truth of their faith may show some of these warning signs. (Go deeper on page 128.)

TRACES OF DEPTH	WARNING SIGNS
❏ balances knowing God and knowing about God ❏ able to communicate faith story ❏ has spiritual mentors ❏ honest (especially about doubt or unknowns) ❏ humble ❏ willingness to learn/teachable ❏ has a recognizable faith ❏ lovingly holds that Christ is the only way ❏ speaks truth in love ❏ high value for the Bible	❏ combative/argumentative ❏ unteachable ❏ believes all opinions on God are true ❏ thinks they have it all figured out ❏ is okay with many higher powers as true ❏ disregards the Bible ❏ derailed by doubt ❏ cannot articulate their faith ❏ beliefs are easily swayed ❏ lacks spiritual mentoring

COMMUNITY: Students who are deeply rooted in their connection with the community of Christ show some of these traces of depth. Students who struggle to be a part of Christian community may display some of these warning signs. (Go deeper on page 130.)

TRACES OF DEPTH	WARNING SIGNS
❏ has many kinds of relationships (mentor, accountability, mentee, outreach) ❏ peacemaker ❏ encourager ❏ submits to spiritual authority ❏ inclusive/welcoming ❏ promotes unity in the church/youth group ❏ understands their role to minister to the world ❏ authentic living—represents the church in or outside of the building ❏ knows/uses spiritual gifts ❏ serving in the church	❏ isolation ❏ holding grudges ❏ avoiding ❏ gossip ❏ divisive ❏ exclusive ❏ inconsistent lifestyle/attitude and actions ❏ constant critic ❏ parasitic ❏ expecting church to serve them

9

Prayer:

Answers to prayer:

[   ]

We must assess our thoughts and beliefs
and reckon whether they are moving us
CLOSER TO CONFORMITY TO CHRIST or
farther away from it. —John Ortberg
(The Life You've Always Wanted: Spiritual Disciplines
for Ordinary People)

Student Profile

Name: _____

Family life: _____

_____

Activities: _____

_____

Passionate about: _____

_____

Burdened by: _____

_____

Influenced by: _____

_____

Testimony: _____

_____

Spends free time:

Growth Plan

	PERSONAL GROWTH: How is God working **IN** this student?	MINISTRY GROWTH: How is God working **THROUGH** this student?
Family		
Peers		
Spiritual Gifts & Wiring		
Leadership		

Growth Plan

GROWTH AND GOALS: consider these questions for your student

How can I encourage the work God is doing IN and
THROUGH this student?

How can I challenge this student to grow?

What intentional conversation do I need to have
with this student?

What short term and long term goals do I have for
this student?

DISCIPLESHIP MAP

1. Check the boxes of words or phrases in both columns that represent or describe your student. If you are unsure or don't know this student in a particular area, then feel free to leave the box empty.

2. When you are finished, look at which of the eight areas (Rescue, Identity, and so on) show a lot of depth—many items checked on the left side and few on the right. Consider how you can encourage or support this student in those areas (an encouragement note, text, or even pointing them to an opportunity where they could continue to grow deeper).

3. Next, decipher which of the eight areas is a struggle for your student, where the warning signs are greatly mounted against the traces of depth. Consider how you might challenge and come alongside your student. A great place to start is with prayer (check out the prayer page for each student) and by adding step-by-step goals or challenges to the Growth Plan (page 108).

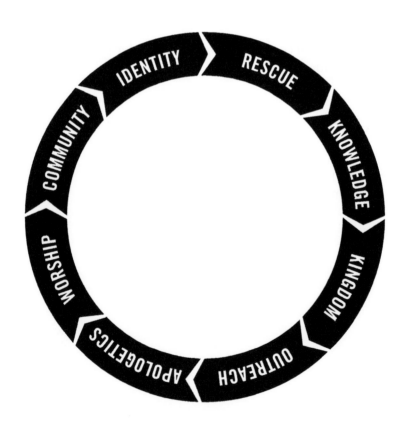

RESCUE: Students who are deeply rooted in their story of being rescued by Christ (salvation and redemption) often show these traces of depth. Students who might not completely grasp this part of discipleship show these warning signs. Check the boxes of words or phrases in both columns that reflect your student's lifestyle.

*For a more complete definition of "Rescue," Scripture verses, as well as some questions to guide a student in their discipleship journey related to this area (and all eight discipleship areas), check out the appendix on page 116.

TRACES OF DEPTH	WARNING SIGNS
❏ passion for evangelism	❏ works-based faith
❏ thankfulness	❏ tries to earn God's love
❏ sacrifices for God and/or others	❏ points fingers
❏ uncompromising	❏ holds onto guilt and shame
❏ lifestyle consistency (same person in all places and circumstances)	❏ holds grudges
	❏ keeps score
❏ confession/repentance is a part of their life	❏ makes excuses
❏ offers forgiveness	❏ acts entitled
❏ shows grace to others and self	❏ blames others often
❏ a realized need for a Savior	❏ takes God's grace for granted
❏ understands consequences of sin	

KNOWLEDGE: Students who are deeply rooted in the truth about who God is and their pursuit of knowing him often show these traces of depth. Students who might hold a false sense of God, or haven't pursued knowing God may display these warning signs. (Go deeper on page 118.)

TRACES OF DEPTH	WARNING SIGNS
❏ a growing awe	❏ growing pride
❏ healthy fear of God	❏ acknowledges more than one God
❏ value for God's Word	
❏ knows the God of the Bible	❏ hides from God
❏ humility/self-awareness	❏ foolishness
❏ growing love/desire to know him	❏ lacks value for God's word
❏ worshipful lifestyle	❏ apathy
❏ God is a part of decisions	❏ seeks beyond God
❏ relationship with God exists beyond the church walls	❏ anger at God
❏ reflects wisdom	❏ expects God to have no involvement
	❏ makes him/herself God of their life

10

IDENTITY: Students who are deeply rooted in their identity as God's children often show some of these traces of depth. Students who struggle to know or live out this identity may display some of these warning signs. (Go deeper on page 120.)

TRACES OF DEPTH	WARNING SIGNS
❏ confidence and self-awareness ❏ using spiritual gifts and wiring/personality for the kingdom ❏ consistent lifestyle (same person in all circumstances) ❏ comfortable in their own skin ❏ affirming of others ❏ likes who they are ❏ embraces growth ❏ accepts criticism ❏ honest ❏ accepts and seeks help	❏ puts others down ❏ identity or worth is determined by environment (performance, teams, groups, problems, etc.) ❏ trying to be someone they aren't ❏ fear or insecurity ❏ self-deprecating ❏ consumed with outer appearance ❏ depression/anxiety ❏ works to feed ego or people pleaser ❏ social media identity doesn't match reality ❏ me against the world mentality

KINGDOM: Students who are deeply rooted in their understanding of God's kingdom and who are living from a kingdom perspective often show some of these traces of depth. Students who struggle to embrace this perspective and are wrestling with a worldly or cultural perspective may display some of these warning signs. (Go deeper on page 122.)

TRACES OF DEPTH	WARNING SIGNS
❏ inspired to serve ❏ embracing the last and least ❏ pushes their comfort zone ❏ willing to sacrifice ❏ appreciation for current circumstances ❏ welcoming and inclusive of others ❏ selfless ❏ has a long-term perspective ❏ knows the King ❏ regularly gives without payment (time, money, attention, resources, respect)	❏ driven by materialism ❏ rarely steps outside of comfort zone ❏ one-upmanship ❏ selfish ❏ lives in the moment ❏ sees themselves as king of their life ❏ reckless living ❏ rarely sees ways to serve others ❏ has many "idols" before God ❏ easily overwhelmed by short-term obstacles

OUTREACH: Students who are deeply rooted in their desire and ability to reach the lost show some of these traces of depth. Students who struggle to reach out to the lost may display some of these warning signs. (Go deeper on page 124.)

TRACES OF DEPTH	WARNING SIGNS
❏ inspired to serve ❏ seeks out the lost ❏ willing to share their faith story ❏ burden for the lost ❏ uses current situations as outreach (where and who they already are) ❏ gives sacrificially (time, money, gifts, etc.) ❏ deep value for others (beyond friends) ❏ courageously shares God's truth ❏ has positive influence on the lost ❏ desire for justice in the world	❏ selfish ❏ uses people ❏ does things that devalue people ❏ afraid to talk about spiritual things ❏ patronizing/mocking ❏ makes excuses for not reaching out ❏ fear of judgment ❏ unsure of spiritual truth ❏ apathetic ❏ easily influenced by the lost

WORSHIP: Students who are deeply rooted in a lifestyle of worship show some of these traces of depth. Students who struggle to worship or show adoration may display some of these warning signs. (Go deeper on page 126.)

TRACES OF DEPTH	WARNING SIGNS
❏ faith is part of their whole life ❏ drawn to worship ❏ gives freely/initiates giving ❏ obedience to God ❏ prayer is a staple and spontaneous ❏ comfortable praying in groups/out loud ❏ thankfulness ❏ desire to imitate Christ/God ❏ worships regardless of circumstance ❏ joyful	❏ many idols (things they value higher than God) ❏ showy worship ❏ takes things for granted ❏ many spiritual highs and lows ❏ feeling-based faith/worship ❏ overly critical of worship styles ❏ shallow prayer life ❏ only worships by singing ❏ worship is compartmentalized to church ❏ sacrifices begrudgingly

APOLOGETICS: Students who are deeply rooted in the truths that sustain their faith show some of these traces of depth. Students who struggle to know and own the truth of their faith may show some of these warning signs. (Go deeper on page 128.)

TRACES OF DEPTH	WARNING SIGNS
❏ balances knowing God and knowing about God ❏ able to communicate faith story ❏ has spiritual mentors ❏ honest (especially about doubt or unknowns) ❏ humble ❏ willingness to learn/teachable ❏ has a recognizable faith ❏ lovingly holds that Christ is the only way ❏ speaks truth in love ❏ high value for the Bible	❏ combative/argumentative ❏ unteachable ❏ believes all opinions on God are true ❏ thinks they have it all figured out ❏ is okay with many higher powers as true ❏ disregards the Bible ❏ derailed by doubt ❏ cannot articulate their faith ❏ beliefs are easily swayed ❏ lacks spiritual mentoring

COMMUNITY: Students who are deeply rooted in their connection with the community of Christ show some of these traces of depth. Students who struggle to be a part of Christian community may display some of these warning signs. (Go deeper on page 130.)

TRACES OF DEPTH	WARNING SIGNS
❏ has many kinds of relationships (mentor, accountability, mentee, outreach) ❏ peacemaker ❏ encourager ❏ submits to spiritual authority ❏ inclusive/welcoming ❏ promotes unity in the church/youth group ❏ understands their role to minister to the world ❏ authentic living—represents the church in or outside of the building ❏ knows/uses spiritual gifts ❏ serving in the church	❏ isolation ❏ holding grudges ❏ avoiding ❏ gossip ❏ divisive ❏ exclusive ❏ inconsistent lifestyle/attitude and actions ❏ constant critic ❏ parasitic ❏ expecting church to serve them

Prayer:

Answers to prayer:

APPENDIX

RESCUE:

What is it? We are slaves, held captive by terrible enemies: sin and death. In this fallen, corrupt, and shattered world, we need a rescuer—Jesus, our Savior and Redeemer. In fact, he's the only one who can save us from this mess that started way back with Adam and Eve. He gave his followers freedom from sin and its effects when he took them on at the cross. This freedom comes at a great cost, but it gives us a new life and reconnects us with God forever. And once we've been freed, we have the opportunity to join in the rescue mission for others.

Questions To Go Deeper: *Use these as mentoring or small group questions, or even just as a way to get to know where your student is in this area.*

- What does it mean to be saved?
- What does it mean to be a child of God?
- How would you describe your relationship with Jesus?
- What difference does Jesus' death on the cross and resurrection make in your life?
- If you were explaining to a friend how to follow Christ and be his disciple, what would you say?

Key verses and passages regarding salvation:
"Yet to all who received him, to those who believed in his name, he gave the right to become children of God – children born not of natural descent, nor of human decision or a husband's will, but born of God" (John 1:12–13).

"For God so loved the world that he gave his one and only Son, that whoever believes in him shall not perish but have eternal life. For God did not send his Son into the world to condemn the world, but to save the world through him" (John 3:16–17).

"For the wages of sin is death, but the gift of God is eternal life in Christ Jesus our Lord" (Rom. 6:23).

"For the Son of Man came to seek and to save what was lost" (Luke 19:10).

"That if you confess with your mouth, 'Jesus is Lord,' and believe in your heart that God raised him from the dead, you will be saved. For it is with your heart that you believe and are justified, and it is with your mouth that you confess and are saved" (Rom. 10:9–10).

Go deeper by studying:
* John 3:16–21—Jesus explains salvation to Nicodemus
* Romans 6—(It might be helpful to split this into two studies.)
* Romans 10:1–13—The process of salvation
* Matthew 19:18–26—The wealthy man and the commandments
* Matthew 13:1–23—Parable of the Sower

NOTES:

KNOWLEDGE:

What is it? God is enormous. He's too big, too awesome, and too complicated to wrap our minds around. Yet he wants us to know him. He wants a relationship with us, so he has revealed himself in a number of ways. Creation tells us about God. The world around us is covered in his fingerprints. The Bible tells the story of God's relationship with his people over the centuries. It also gives us names that describe him—Creator, Almighty, Holy One—and metaphors to help us connect with him—Father, Rock, Shepherd. He sent his Son, Jesus, to live on earth as fully God and fully man, "God with us." And he sent the Holy Spirit to comfort us and unite us to him. We will never know everything about God. But in order to become his disciples, we need to know some essential truths about the One we follow.

Questions To Go Deeper: *Use these as mentoring or small group questions, or even just as a way to get to know where your student is at in this area.*

- What are some ways you connect with and get to know God?
- How would you describe God to a friend?
- How important is the Bible to your daily life?
- What role does the Holy Spirit play in your life?

Key verses and passages regarding knowing God:
"All Scripture is God-breathed and is useful for teaching, rebuking, correcting and training in righteousness, so that the man of God may be thoroughly equipped for every good work" (2 Tim. 3:16–17).

"In the same way, the Spirit helps us in our weakness. We do not know what we ought to pray for, but the Spirit himself intercedes for us with groans that words cannot express" (Rom. 8:26).

"Jesus Christ is the same yesterday and today and forever" (Heb. 13:8).

"For God is not a God of disorder but of peace" (1 Cor. 14:33a).

"Righteousness and justice are the foundation of your throne; love and faithfulness go before you" (Ps. 89:14).

"Come near to God and he will come near to you" (James 4:8a).

Go deeper by studying:
* John 1:1–18—The Word and Jesus
* John 16:7–15—The Holy Spirit
* Mark 12:28–34—The greatest commandments
* Colossians 1:15–23—Jesus Christ as King
* Isaiah 40—The power of God

NOTES:

IDENTITY:

What is it? It started with Adam and Eve. God created humans in his own image, unique in all creation. While God declared his other creations "good," he identified humans as "very good." Then sin entered the picture, and all people developed a warped version of their original identity, a sinner's nature in need of major restoration. Christ died on the cross and rose again to offer us a new identity, even better than the first. He took on our sin and shame so we could take on his righteousness. He identifies with us so we can find our identity in him—a redeemed identity.

Questions To Go Deeper: *Use these as mentoring or small group questions, or even just as a way to get to know where your student is at in this area.*

- How would your friends describe who you are?
- How would God describe who you are?
- What difference does it make in your daily life to know that you are God's child?
- What's the difference between your identity with Christ and your identity before Christ?

Key verses and passages regarding identity in Christ:
"So God created man in his own image, in the image of God he created him; male and female he created them" (Gen. 1:27).

"Therefore, if anyone is in Christ, he is a new creation; the old has gone, the new has come!" (2 Cor. 5:17).

"Then Jesus said to his disciples, 'Whoever wants to be my disciple must deny themselves and take up their cross and follow me'" (Matt. 16:24).

"But our citizenship is in heaven. And we eagerly await a Savior from there, the Lord Jesus Christ" (Phil. 3:20).

"For God did not give us a spirit of timidity, but a spirit of power, of love and of self-discipline" (2 Tim. 1:7).

Go deeper by studying:
* Ephesians 1:1-14—Adopted into God's family
* Romans 8:1-17—Freedom as God's child
* Galatians 5:16-26—Living by the Spirit versus sinful nature
* 1 Corinthians 12:1-11—Spiritual gifts
* Psalm 139—Uniquely created by God

NOTES:

KINGDOM:

What is it? Simply put, the kingdom of God is wherever God is King. It's not a specific place on earth or in heaven. It's everywhere God reigns and his subjects honor him as their ruler. When you follow Christ, you acknowledge him as the Lord of your life. You call him King. At that point you begin living in the kingdom of God. In his kingdom, human logic doesn't always compute. The laws of living are different, based on God's greater wisdom. Jesus tells us that "the first shall be last, and the last shall be first," and "riches" are more than just "money." In God's kingdom the least are priceless, peace trumps power, and justice wins in the end.

Questions To Go Deeper: *Use these as mentoring or small group questions, or even just as a way to get to know where your student is at in this area.*

- What kinds of things are valuable in God's kingdom?
- What kinds of things are valuable to the world?
- What does it mean to have a kingdom perspective on life?
- The kingdom of God is where God is King, where he is Lord. Is he Lord of your life?

Key verses and passages regarding the Kingdom:
"Once, having been asked by the Pharisees when the kingdom of God would come, Jesus replied, 'The kingdom of God does not come with your careful observation, nor will people say, 'Here it is,' or 'There it is,' because the kingdom of God is within you'" (Luke 17:20–21).

"The Lord has established his throne in heaven, and his kingdom rules over all" (Ps. 103:19).

"Do not store up for yourselves treasures on earth where moth and rust destroy, and where thieves break in and steal. But store up for yourselves treasures in heaven, where moth and rust do not destroy, and where thieves do not break in and steal" (Matt. 6:19–20).

"For the kingdom of God is not a matter of talk but of power" (1 Cor. 4:20).

"Sitting down, Jesus called the Twelve and said, 'If anyone wants to be first, he must be the very last and servant of all'" (Mark 9:35).

Go deeper by studying:
* Matthew 5:1–16—The Beatitudes
* Matthew 13:1–10; 18–23—Parable of the Sower
* Mark 9:33–37—The first will become last
* James 1:1–12—Trials and perseverance
* Matthew 6:25–34—Kingdom perspective

NOTES:

OUTREACH:

What is it? Before he returned to his Father in heaven, Jesus gave his followers one last command: to spread the good news of his death and resurrection—the gospel—to the whole world. That's a daunting task. But if we truly understand the joy we have as followers of Jesus, we'll realize that sharing this joy is the greatest act of love we can show another person. When we become members of Christ's body of believers, the story doesn't end. That's just the beginning! Now we get to join in a remarkable mission to care for the least, to love other people, and to share Jesus as Lord wherever we go.

Questions to go deeper: *Use these as mentoring or small group questions, or even just as a way to get to know where your student is at in this area.*

- What's the best way to reach people for Christ?
- How would you explain your faith to a friend who didn't know Jesus?
- What does serving others have to do with following Christ? Why?
- Who reached out to you and showed you how to follow Christ?

Key verses and passages regarding Outreach:
"Therefore go and make disciples of all nations, baptizing them in the name of the Father and of the Son and of the Holy Spirit" (Matt. 28:19).

"How, then, can they call on the one they have not believed in? And how can they believe in the one of the whom they have not heard? And how can they hear without someone preaching to them? And how can they preach unless they are sent?" (Rom. 10:14–15a).

"Then he said to his disciples, 'The harvest is plentiful but the workers are few. Ask the Lord of the harvest, therefore, to send out workers into his harvest field'" (Matt. 10:37–38).

"In the same way, let your light shine before men, that they may see your good deeds and praise your Father in heaven" (Matt. 5:16).

"You, my brothers, were called to be free. But do not use your freedom to indulge the sinful nature; rather, serve one another in love. The entire law is summed up in a single command: 'Love your neighbor as yourself'" (Gal. 5:13–14).

"The King will reply, 'I tell you the truth, whatever you did for one of the least of these brothers of mine, you did for me'" (Matt. 25:40).

Go deeper by studying:
* 2 Corinthians 5:14–21—We are Christ's ambassadors
* Luke 10:25–37—Parable of the Good Samaritan
* Matthew 28:16–20—The Great Commission
* John 13:1–17—Jesus washes the disciples' feet
* John 4:1–30—The woman at the well

NOTES:

WORSHIP:

What is it? We sing because we worship. We pray because we worship. We dance because we worship. By themselves, these things are not all that special and can even be self-serving. But when they are done in response to God, they become worship played out in our lives. You see, worship is a lifestyle. It's how you go about your day, and it happens when you get a vivid glimpse of God, his power, and his majesty. In the Bible, anyone who has a close encounter with God can't help but marvel at his glory. The angels, his messengers, are in a constant state of worship. We, too, can express a life of worship by encountering God on a daily basis.

Questions to go deeper: *Use these as mentoring or small group questions, or even just as a way to get to know where your student is at in this area.*

- How do you worship God?
- Why do you worship God?
- What about God is worthy of adoration (worship)?
- What are the ways you get to know God and connect with him?

Key verses and passages regarding Worship:
"Give praise to the Lord, proclaim his name; make known among the nations what he has done" (Ps. 105:1).

"Therefore, I urge you, brothers, in view of God's mercy, to offer your bodies as living sacrifices, holy and pleasing to God—this is your spiritual act of worship" (Rom. 12:2).

"Love the Lord your God with all your heart and with all your soul and with all your strength" (Deut. 6:5).

"Through Jesus, therefore, let us continually offer to God a sacrifice of praise—the fruit of lips that confess his name" (Heb. 13:15).

"Put to death, therefore, whatever belongs to your earthly nature: sexual immorality, impurity, lust, evil desires and greed, which is idolatry" (Col. 3:5).

"These people honor me with their lips, but their hearts are far from me. They worship me in vain; their teachings are but rules taught by men" (Matt. 15:8–9).

Go deeper by studying:
*Psalm 150—Adoration through music
*Mark 8:34–38—Sacrifice
*Matthew 22:34-40—The greatest commandment
*James 5:13–18—Prayer
*Philippians 4:4–9—Worship with thoughts

NOTES:

APOLOGETICS:

What is it? The Bible encourages us to defend our faith: "Always be prepared to give an answer to everyone who asks you to give the reason for the hope that you have. But do this with gentleness and respect" (1 Pet. 3:15). That's the point of apologetics—to explain our hope in Christ to others. We shouldn't do this in an overbearing way, as if we're hitting people over the head. On the other hand, we shouldn't detach ourselves from the rest of the world, too concerned with our own safety or offending someone that we never impact others. If we're confident in the truth God has given us, then we won't be ashamed to respectfully engage our culture in productive ways.

Questions to go deeper: *Use these as mentoring or small group questions, or even just as a way to get to know where your student is at in this area.*

- Why do you follow Christ?
- What's your testimony?
- How do you know that Jesus is real?
- What do you do with doubt?

Key verses and passages regarding Apologetics:
"Jesus answered, 'I am the way and the truth and the life. No one comes to the Father except through me'" (John 14:6).

"But in your hearts set apart Christ as Lord. Always be prepared to give an answer to everyone who asks you to give the reason for the hope that you have. But do this with gentleness and respect" (1 Pet. 3:15).

"Test everything. Hold on to the good. Avoid every kind of evil" (1 Thes. 5:21–22).

"The grass withers and the flowers fall, but the word of our God stands forever" (Isa. 40:8).

"Do your best to present yourself to God as one approved, a workman who does not need to be ashamed and who correctly handles the word of truth" (2 Tim. 2:15).

"Accept the one whose faith is weak, without quarreling over disputable matters" (Rom. 14:1).

Go deeper by studying:
* 1 John 4:1–6—Test for the truth
* James 2:14–26—Faith and works
* Acts 17:16–34—Paul and the philosophers
* Galatians 1—Warning against changing the gospel of Christ
* 1 Corinthians 15:1–23—Why the resurrection matters

NOTES:

COMMUNITY:

What is it? We weren't created to be alone. Our emotional, physical, and spiritual well-being depends on deep, loving relationships with other people. But the world builds walls between us, painfully isolating us from other human beings. That's the beauty of the church. When we start following Jesus, we form a bond with the others who call him Lord. Do you ever feel outcast, lonely, inferior, ashamed, or disconnected? God has created a family for you. They are his people, and they will help you grow in another essential connection—with God.

Questions to go deeper: *Use these as mentoring or small group questions, or even just as a way to get to know where your student is at in this area.*

- Who is the most influential person in your life? Why?
- What role does church play in your spiritual life?
- Do the people closest to you share your faith? Why or why not?
- Can you follow Christ alone? Why or why not?

Key verses and passages regarding Community:

"Religion that God our Father accepts as pure and faultless is this: to look after orphans and widows in their distress and to keep oneself from being polluted by the world" (James 1:27).

"Join with others in following my example, brothers, and take note of those who live according to the pattern we gave you" (Phil. 3:17).

"Make every effort to live in peace with all men and to be holy; without holiness no one will see the Lord. See to it that no one misses the grace of God and that no bitter root grows up to cause trouble and defile many" (Heb. 12:14–15).

"Brothers if someone is caught in a sin, you who are spiritual should restore him gently. But watch yourself, or you also may be tempted" (Gal. 6:1).

"But you are a chosen people, a royal priesthood, a holy nation, a people belonging to God, that you may declare the praises of him who called you out of darkness into his wonderful light" (1 Pet. 2:9).

Go deeper by studying:
* Colossians 3:12–17—How to live in community
* James 2:1–13—Favoritism and judgment
* Acts 2:42–47—The community of the early church
* Romans 12—The church is a body with many parts
* Ephesians 1:15–23—Christ is the head of the church

NOTES:

Learn more about Deep Discipleship at

www.leadertreks.com/deep_disicpleship

Deep Discipleship is a discipleship plan for your youth ministry. It's designed to work within your current programming through easy-to-use, in-depth Bible study lessons. We've identified eight spiritual principles needed to produce rooted disciples of Jesus. Each lesson builds on the last to keep discipleship at the center of your student ministry. Week after week you will teach solid biblical truth paired with engaging experiences that encourage students to exercise their growing faith.

In Deep Discipleship, students are also equipped with *I Am a Disciple: A 40-Day Discipleship Journal* to help students go deeper into their journey with Christ. Each day, students will experience, learn about, and put into practice one of the eight principles (roots) of discipleship.

I Am a Disciple contains 40 days of:
>> Bible Studies
>> Challenges
>> Thought-provoking Experiences
>> Hard Questions
>> Insights into the Marks of a Disciple
>> And Mentor Pages to use with
    someone like you!

Making Disciples...Developing Leaders
www.leadertreks.com 877-502-0699

TPS 162471